Overview of Drug Issues in Ireland 2000
A Resource Document

Rosalyn Moran
Mary O'Brien
Lucy Dillon
Eimear Farrell
of the
Drug Misuse Research Division

With input from Paula Mayock
University of Dublin, Trinity College

The Drug Misuse Research Division
The Health Research Board
Dublin
2001

Citation:

Moran, R., O'Brien, M., Dillon, L. & Farrell, E., with Mayock, P. (2001)
Overview of Drug Issues in Ireland 2000: A Resource Document. Dublin:
The Health Research Board.

Published by:
Drug Misuse Research Division
The Health Research Board
73 Lower Baggot Street
Dublin 2
Ireland
Tel: 00-353-(0)1-6761176
Fax: 00-353-(0)1-6611856
Email: dmrd@hrb.ie
Web: www.hrb.ie

ISBN: 1-903669-01-4

CONTENTS

LIST OF TABLES

LIST OF FIGURES

LIST OF ABBREVIATIONS

ADHD	Attention Deficit Hyperactivity Disorder
ADM	Area Development Management Ltd
A&E	Accident & Emergency
AIDS	Acquired Immunodeficiency Syndrome
BMW	Border, Midlands and Western region
CAB	Criminal Assets Bureau
CARP	Community Addiction Response Programme
CDB	County/City Development Board
COREPER	Committee of the Permanent Representatives (of the member states of the EU)
CSO	Central Statistics Office
DofHC	Department of Health and Children
DofTSR	Department of Tourism, Sport and Recreation
DAP	Drug Awareness Programme
DDRAM	Drug Dependence: Risk and Monitoring
DMRD	Drug Misuse Research Division
DPP	Director of Public Prosecutions
DSM	Diagnostic and Statistical Manual of Mental Disorders
EDDRA	European Database on Demand Reduction Activities
EDU	Europol Drugs Unit
EHB	Eastern Health Board
EMCDDA	European Monitoring Centre for Drugs and Drug Addiction
ERHA	Eastern Regional Health Authority
ESPAD	European Schools Survey Project on Alcohol and Other Drugs

EU	European Union
Europol	European Police Office
GMR	General Mortality Register
GNDU	Garda National Drugs Unit
GP	General Practitioner
HBSC	Health Behaviours in School-Aged Children
HIPE	Hospital Inpatient Enquiry database
HIV	Human Immunodeficiency Virus
HRB	Health Research Board
ICD	International Classification of Diseases
ICT	Information and Communications Technologies
IDU	Injecting drug user
IVDU	Intravenous drug user
JLO	Juvenile Liaison Officer
KAB1	Drug-Rrelated Knowledge, Attitudes and Beliefs, a survey of the general adult population in Ireland, published by the Drug Misuse Research Division
KAB2	An expanded study, following KAB1, to be published by the Drug Misuse Research Division
KDI	Kilkenny Drugs Initiative
LDTF	Local Drug Task Force
MDA	Misuse of Drugs Acts, 1977 & 1984
MDMA	Methylenedioxy methamphetamine (Ecstasy)
MHB	Midland Health Board
NA	Narcotics Anonymous
NACD	National Advisory Committee on Drugs
NAPS	National Anti-Poverty Strategy
NCDP	National Community Development Programme
NDP	National Development Plan
NDTRS	National Drug Treatment Reporting System
NEHB	North Eastern Health Board
NEP	Needle Exchange Programme
NIMBY	Not In My Back Yard
NPIRS	National Psychiatric Inpatient Reporting System
NUI	National University of Ireland
NWHB	North Western Health Board
PESAT	European Foundation of Drug Helplines
PPF	Programme for Prosperity and Fairness
REITOX	European Information Network on Drugs and Drug Addiction

S&E	Southern and Eastern region
SHB	Southern Health Board
SLÁN	Survey of Lifestyle, Attitudes and Nutrition
SMI	Strategic Management Initiative
S.P.H.E.	Social, Personal and Health Education programme
STD	Sexually-transmitted disease
UCD	University College, Dublin
UN	United Nations
VEC	Vocational Education Committee
VIP	Vital Information Pack
WHB	Western Health Board
WHO	World Health Organisation
YPFSF	Young People's Facilities and Services Fund

ACKNOWLEDGEMENTS

This report is very much the result of collaborative work within and outside the Drug Misuse Research Division. We in the Drug Misuse Research Division would like to thank very sincerely those people working in the drugs area who gave generously of their time to inform us about recent developments in their areas of work. It is not possible to name all these people but the agencies with which they are affiliated are acknowledged as follows:

Department of Tourism, Sport and Recreation
Department of Health and Children
Department of Justice, Equality and Law Reform
Department of Social ,Community and Family Affairs
Department of Education and Science
An Garda Síochána – Irish police force
Forensic Science Laboratory
Health Boards and Drug Treatment Facilities
Mental Health Research Division of Health Research Board
Centre for Health Promotion Studies, National University of Ireland, Galway.

Thanks also to members of the judiciary, voluntary and community groups and academic researchers in universities and research institutes who provided inputs for the report.

The authors would like to thank all those who provided comments on the report, in particular the internal and external reviewers – personnel from the Department of Tourism, Sport and Recreation, the Department of Health and Children, the Department of Justice, Equality and Law Reform – and our colleagues in the Drug Misuse Research Division, Tracy Kelleher and Paul Cahill.

Particular thanks are due to Brigid Pike who edited the document. Brigid contributed greatly to the readability of the document.

Finally many thanks to Mary Dunne who put the final touches to the document and managed its production.

Rosalyn Moran
Mary O'Brien
Lucy Dillon
Eimear Farrell

May 2001

GENERAL INTRODUCTION

ROSALYN MORAN

The Overview

This publication provides an overview of issues related to drug misuse in Ireland, focusing on information available up to mid-2000. The term 'drug misuse', as used in this report, refers to the taking of a legal and/or illegal drug that harms the physical, mental or social well being of the individual, the group or society.

A general overview of the situation in Ireland regarding different aspects of the drugs phenomenon is presented. The content is descriptive rather than analytic. The authors envisage that the document will be used as a resource document. Much of the information presented is not readily available in the Irish context; thus, this volume, which gathers a wide range of information together, should be of use to individuals and groups interested in the drugs area in Ireland. The topics covered in the seven chapters are as follows.

Chapter 1 overviews Irish Government strategy in relation to illegal drugs and the main mechanisms involved in the implementation of the strategy. Budget and funding arrangements in the drugs area are outlined within the context of the National Development Programme 2000–2006 (NDP, 2000).

Chapter 2 describes the body of legislation directly or indirectly relevant to the control of drugs, beginning with the Poisons (Ireland) Act, 1870 and concluding with the Criminal Justice (Theft and Fraud Offences) Bill, 2000. Commentary on some of the implications of the most recent changes in legislation is provided. The organisation of the enforcement agencies and their interrelationships are presented. This is followed by an overview of the processes involved in drug law enforcement, up to procedures for sentencing. Finally, some recent developments in activities in the law enforcement area, related to both supply and demand reduction, are summarised.

Chapter 3 describes the results of studies, which have researched the use of drugs by different groups in Ireland, e.g. general population surveys, and school and youth surveys. Caution in the extraction of general trends is advocated, given the different objectives and methodologies used by different studies. The need for regular surveys, using comparable methodologies, which would allow trends over time to be monitored, is stressed. For meaningful interpretation, such surveys should, where possible, be comparable nationally as well as in the wider European context.

Chapter 4 provides an overview of clients who present for drug treatment in Ireland – the characteristics of such users, their patterns of use and trends in use and in risk behaviour. Much of the data informing this chapter comes from the National Drug Treatment Reporting System (NDTRS), based in the Drug Misuse Research Division (DMRD) of the Health Research Board (HRB). Patterns and trends in relation to drug-related infectious diseases (e.g. HIV, AIDS, hepatitis B and C infection), psychiatric co-morbidity and drug-related mortality are presented.

Chapter 5 reports results of studies that examined certain social issues associated with drug misuse, e.g. housing, homelessness, public nuisance, and community problems. The need for more research into the social and economic costs of drug misuse is highlighted. Findings from the first national survey of public attitudes to drugs, drug users, drug policy etc., carried out by the DMRD, are discussed. Some drug-related issues, which have been the subject of recent public debate, are outlined.

Chapter 6 overviews drug-related data gathered by law enforcement agencies such as the Gardaí and the Customs Service. Available information on charges for drug offences, the number and quantities of drugs seizures, and the price and purity of drugs seized is presented. Sources of supply and trafficking patterns are briefly covered. The need for research into drug–related law enforcement issues and drug-related crime in the Irish context, is highlighted.

Chapter 7 describes a large number of demand reduction programmes or interventions under way in the Irish context, which fall under the general headings – prevention, harm minimisation and treatment. The table of contents provides a detailed list of headings, which can guide the reader to programmes relating to specific types of interest; for example, Section 7.3.5 on Telephone Helplines details three specific telephone helpline services. The need to develop a culture of evaluation around the development of programmes aiming to reduce the demand for drugs is highlighted, as is the need for on-going training and support for such evaluation. This chapter also overviews the training courses available in Ireland in the drugs area by describing the *Directory of Training Courses in Drug Misuse*, which was commissioned by the Department of Tourism, Sport and Recreation (Department of Tourism, Sport and Recreation, 1999). In addition, some of the main means for the dissemination of information on drug misuse in Ireland are noted – DrugNet Ireland, EDDRA, and the new National Documentation Centre on Drug Misuse, located in the DMRD of the HRB. This new national resource, established under the National Advisory Committee on Drugs (NACD), will provide a major source of information on literature in the drugs misuse area, to interested individuals and agencies.

EMCDDA Guidelines

The content and structure of this document adhere in large part to guidelines provided by the European Monitoring Centre for Drugs and Drug Addiction (EMCDDA)[1] to the DMRD of the HRB. The DMRD is the designated Irish Focal Point for the REITOX network, i.e. the European Information Network on Drugs and Drug Addiction. These 'Focal Points' are national centres of expertise on drug-related issues in the member states of the European Union (EU). On an annual basis, Focal Points in each member state draw up an annual report on the national drug problem, under contract with the EMCDDA, using these guidelines.

The EMCDDA uses information from reports from the member states when compiling the *Annual Report on the State of the Drugs Problem in the European Union*.[2] The Europe-wide reports are available on the EMCDDA and the linked HRB websites.[3] The HRB edits and publishes the contributory Irish national report every three years (O'Brien & Moran, 1998).

---

1   The EMCDDA is an EU institution providing information concerning drugs and drug addiction and their consequences. The EMCDDA works to improve the comparability of drug-related data in the member states, to disseminate information, and co-operate with international bodies dealing with drug-related issues.
2   See, for example, EMCDDA (2000). *Annual Report on the State of the Drugs Problem in the European Union 2000*. Luxembourg: Office for Official Publications of the European Communities. Editions have also been published for the years 1996, 1997, 1998 and 1999.
3   See www.emcdda.org and www.hrb.ie

The EMCDDA guidelines for the 2000 annual national report included coverage of some 'key issues or topics', which were agreed by the countries of the EU and the EMCDDA to be of particular interest. These key issues were written as chapters for the EMCDDA report and will be published separately in the near future (Moran, Dillon, O'Brien, Mayock & Farrell, forthcoming). The forthcoming publication, will cover the following topics:

- implementation of national drugs strategy (Moran);
- overview of the current situation in Ireland in relation to drug-related infectious diseases, including HIV, hepatitis B and hepatitis C (Dillon & O'Brien);
- a review of Irish literature and official information sources on cocaine use, along with the presentation of findings from a small exploratory study of cocaine users (Mayock); and
- a review of Irish literature on women, children and drug use, first prepared for the 1999 national report[4] (Farrell).

The time and resources allocated to the present report were, of necessity, limited, so no claim to complete coverage is made. Accordingly, the report is presented as a 'resource document' and comments on the report are welcome.[5] Welcome in particular are updates to the information provided, since a similar report will be produced each year by the DMRD for the EMCDDA.

References

EMCDDA (1996). *Annual Report on the State of the Drugs Problem in the European Union 1996.* Luxembourg: Office for Official Publications of the European Communities.

EMCDDA (1997). *Annual Report on the State of the Drugs Problem in the European Union 1997.* Luxembourg: Office for Official Publications of the European Communities.

EMCDDA (1998). *Annual Report on the State of the Drugs Problem in the European Union 1998.* Luxembourg: Office for Official Publications of the European Communities.

---

4   See Moran, R., O'Brien, M., Farrell, E. & Dillon, L. (1999). 'National Report on Drug Issues Ireland.' Internal document. Dublin: Drug Misuse Research Division, The Health Research Board.
5   Please send comments to Head of Division, DMRD, Health Research Board, 73 Lower Baggot Street, Dublin 2. Fax number – 00 353 1 6611856, or email – dmrd@hrb.ie

EMCDDA (1999). *Annual Report on the State of the Drugs Problem in the European Union 1999.* Luxembourg: Office for Official Publications of the European Communities.

EMCDDA (2000). *Annual Report on the State of the Drugs Problem in the European Union 2000.* Luxembourg: Office for Official Publications of the European Communities.

O'Brien, M. & Moran, R. (1998). *Overview of Drug Issues in Ireland, 1997.* Dublin: Drug Misuse Research Division, The Health Research Board.

Moran, R., O'Brien, M., Farrell, E. & Dillon, L. (1999). 'National Report on Drug Issues Ireland'. Internal document. Dublin: Drug Misuse Research Division, The Health Research Board.

Moran, R., Dillon, L., O'Brien, M., Mayock, P. & Farrell, E. (forthcoming). *A Collection of Papers on Drug Issues in Ireland: Implementation of drug strategy, drug-related infectious diseases, cocaine use and women, children and drug use.* Dublin: Drug Misuse Research Division, The Health Research Board.

NDP (2000). *Ireland, National Development Plan 2000 – 2006.* Dublin: The Stationery Office.

Department of Tourism, Sport and Recreation (1999). *Directory of Training Courses in Drug Misuse.* Dublin: The Stationery Office.

CHAPTER 1

DRUGS STRATEGY, BUDGET AND FUNDING ARRANGEMENTS

ROSALYN MORAN

1.1 Introduction

This chapter describes Irish government strategy in relation to illegal drugs, the main institutional mechanisms to implement this strategy, and the budget and funding arrangements to resource implementation. A companion volume will describe the main programmes and initiatives under way (Moran, Dillon, O'Brien, Mayock & Farrell, forthcoming). The chapter focuses on developments up to mid-2000, and its format follows, in large part, guidelines provided by the European Monitoring Centre for Drugs and Drug Addiction (EMCDDA) (see General Introduction).

1.2 Drugs Strategy

Significant changes have occurred in Irish society over the last six years. Foremost among these are dynamic economic growth, improved living standards, ending of large-scale emigration, improved employment opportunities, and the emergence of a young, educated population. Amid these positive developments, however, there exist pockets of poverty, homelessness, drug addiction and disaffection, particularly among young people in certain urban areas (Inter-Departmental Committee, 1998–1999: 56). The Government, recognising the inequitable distribution of societal resources, has made social inclusion a policy priority, and on foot of wide social partnership arrangements such as the National Development Plan (NDP, 2000), the Programme for Prosperity and Fairness (PPF, 2000), and the National Anti-Poverty Strategy (NAPS, 1998/99; 1999/2000), has allocated much-needed financial resources to combat poverty and social exclusion.

The Government's approach to the drugs problem is embedded in this broad social inclusion framework (Drug Misuse Research Division, 1999). The effects of social exclusion are seen 'to contribute to the deep rooted and intractable problems of serious drug misuse' (Flood, 1999). An integrated inter-agency approach to tackling these problems has been put in place; power to tackle social exclusion is being devolved to local and regional authorities, through the development of appropriate structures; and local community participation in the formulation and implementation of policy is being nurtured and resourced.

Ireland's National Drugs Strategy is currently being framed. It is being developed in the context of various international and EU agreements, for example the Political Declaration on the Guiding Principles of Drugs Demand Reduction (UN Special Session on Drugs, held in New York, 1998)[1] the UN Conventions on Narcotic Drugs and Psychotropic Substances,[2] the EU Action Plan on Drugs 2000 – 2004 (Commission of the European Communities, 1999), and the EU Drugs Strategy 2000 – 2004 (CORDROGUE 64, 1999). The development of Ireland's National Drugs Strategy has also involved extensive consultation, including public fora in a number of centres throughout the country. The new strategy is due to be launched in early to mid 2001.

Since 1996 the Irish Government's drugs strategy has been underpinned by the findings, recommendations and policies established by the two reports of the Ministerial Task Force on Measures to Reduce the Demand for Drugs (1996 & 1997). The overall aim of the Government's current drugs strategy is to provide an effective, integrated response to the problems posed by drug misuse, and to work in partnership with the communities most affected by the drugs problem in tackling the issues involved.

---

1   At a UN Special Session on Drugs, held in New York in 1998, a Political Declaration on the Guiding Principles of Drug Demand Reduction was adopted. It put an onus on every member state to have in place a comprehensive drugs policy and outline of how targets are to be achieved over the period 2000 to 2008.

2   Single Convention on Narcotic Drugs, 1961, as amended by the 1972 Protocol Amending the Single Convention on Narcotic Drugs, 1961; the Convention on Psychotropic Substances, 1971; and the UN Convention against the Illicit Traffic in Narcotic Drugs and Psychotropic Substances, 1988. The conventions may be accessed through the website – www.incb.org/e/conv/

The key objectives of the Irish Government's current drugs strategy are to:

- reduce the number of people turning to drugs in the first instance, through comprehensive education and prevention programmes;
- provide appropriate treatment and aftercare for those dependent on drugs;
- have appropriate mechanisms at national and local level aimed at reducing the supply of illicit drugs; and
- ensure that an appropriate level of accurate and timely information is available to inform the response to the problem.

In line with these overall aims and objectives, four basic principles underpin the Government's strategy.

- It is recognised that an effective strategy must encompass a range of responses, which not only address the consequences of drug misuse, but also address its causes.
- The response to the drugs problem must take account of the different levels of drug misuse being experienced around the country. Illicit drug use, particularly of drugs such as cannabis and ecstasy, is a nationwide phenomenon. However, heroin abuse, in view of its public health implications and close association with crime, is currently seen as the most pressing aspect of the problem. Therefore, the areas experiencing the highest levels of heroin abuse require a specific targeted response.
- All agencies with a role in responding to the drugs problem need to work together, to ensure that their individual programmes and services are delivered in a coherent, integrated manner.
- There is considerable knowledge and experience to be found in the communities experiencing the highest levels of drug misuse, and these communities must have an opportunity to participate in the design and delivery of responses to the drugs problem in their areas (Flood, 1999).

At the level of the individual, the objective of drugs policy in Ireland is to maintain people in, and restore misusers to, a drug-free lifestyle. However, in practice, it is acknowledged that the latter is not an option for a number of citizens in the short term. Accordingly, a pragmatic approach is taken, and the importance of the minimisation of risk, or harm reduction, is stressed in treatment and in a number of education and rehabilitation programmes. The emphasis on harm reduction has grown in line with the growing concern about the public health implications of the increase in the incidence of AIDS/HIV and hepatitis B and C infections.

The Government's drugs strategy involves a range of responses, addressing both the causes and the consequences of drug misuse. The Government's response may be characterised as supporting general initiatives to promote social inclusion, and also specific initiatives within the social inclusion framework that target drug-related problems. The general initiatives target issues seen as contributing to the drugs problem, for example, unemployment and social deprivation (Drug Misuse Research Division, 1999). Such programmes provide scope for agencies and communities affected by the drugs problem to avail of financial and other resources to tackle the broader problems associated with drug misuse in their communities.

The Government's specific response to the drugs problem focuses on two major initiatives – the Local Drug Task Forces (LDTFs) and the Young People's Facilities and Services Fund (YPFSF). The LDTFs were established to provide a strategic local response, by statutory, community and voluntary sectors, in areas where drug misuse is a serious problem. There are twelve LDTFs in Dublin, one in Cork, and one in Bray. The YPFSF was established by the Government in 1998 to assist in the development of youth facilities, including sport and recreation facilities and services, in disadvantaged areas, where a significant drugs problem exists or has the potential to develop. The aim of the fund is to attract 'at-risk' young people into these facilities and activities, thereby diverting them from the dangers of substance misuse. A more detailed description of these two major initiatives is given in Moran *et al.* (forthcoming).

In addition to the LDTFs and the YPFSF, which are largely focused on urban areas, where the drugs problem is most acute, Government strategy has begun to address the drugs problem on a nationwide basis. It has begun to address the use of so-called 'recreational drugs', such as cannabis and ecstasy, particularly among young people. There is a growing recognition that illegal drugs, particularly cannabis and ecstasy, are readily accessible in towns and rural areas throughout the country and, along with alcohol, are becoming an increasingly common feature of recreational activity among certain categories of youth (Kelleher, forthcoming; O'Brien & Moran, forthcoming). Pockets of heroin use in some larger rural towns have also been reported. Regional drugs co-ordinators have been appointed to assist the regional health boards in developing appropriate programmes and services, mostly in relation to drugs awareness, education, prevention, and also treatment and rehabilitation when needed. Since 1992 these programmes and services have been in receipt of a specific financial allocation from the Department of Health and Children. This allocation represents additional funding for regional health boards to respond to the drugs problem.

Regional drugs co-ordinators also have a role in co-ordinating the responses of agencies at a local level. At the request of the Department of Health and Children, all health boards now have co-ordination structures in place, which work with varying degrees of success and involvement from other agencies and groups (Department of Health and Children, 2000). Thus, a number of the regional health boards have set up regional co-ordinating committees in their areas, which work in partnership with other relevant agencies in developing a co-ordinated response to the drugs problem, having regard to the needs of their particular regions.

The Government's strategy involves a number of major initiatives to tackle the drugs problem from the supply side (see Chapters 2 and 6). Legislation has been introduced over the past few years to increase significantly the powers of the Gardaí and other authorities in tackling organised crime and drug dealing. But agencies working on the supply side have recognised that supply reduction measures must be accompanied by demand reduction measures, and these have now become an increasingly important aspect of the work of law enforcement agencies. Chapter 7 describes some projects on demand reduction, which represent interventions in the criminal justice system. A summary of recent initiatives in the criminal justice area can be found in Chapter 2.

1.3 Institutional Mechanisms

The institutional mechanisms to implement the National Drugs Strategy, not surprisingly, overlap with the mechanisms to promote social inclusion in general. Foremost among these mechanisms is the Cabinet Committee on Social Inclusion, which gives political direction to the Government's social inclusion policies. This committee receives input from the Inter-Departmental Group on the National Drugs Strategy and the National Drugs Strategy Team. The relevant government departments and agencies are represented on these two bodies. The Inter-Departmental Group on the National Drugs Strategy includes senior-level representation from government departments and representatives from the National Drugs Strategy Team. The National Drugs Strategy Team also includes two non-government representatives, one each from the community and the voluntary sectors.

The Inter-Departmental Group on the National Drugs Strategy addresses issues in the drugs area with an inter-departmental dimension. The National Drugs Strategy Team plays a central role in overseeing the implementation of the Government's drugs strategy. It also plays a role at an operational level, for example monitoring the work of the LDTFs. The team was established on the principles outlined in the Strategic Management Initiative (SMI) for addressing issues that cut across the remit of a number of government departments and agencies.

Finally, the LDTFs provide a strategic locally-based response by the statutory, community and voluntary sectors to the drugs problem in the areas worst affected. The National Assessment Committee and Development Groups, established under the YPFSF, are also involved at the implementation level. A full description of the LDTFs and YPFSF, and their programmes, is provided in Moran *et al.* (forthcoming).

Preliminary arrangements have also been made to advance the objective of regional devolution, as outlined, for example, in the NDP. Accordingly, the LDTFs and area-based partnership companies are to work with the newly-appointed Directors of Community and Enterprise and the County/City Development Boards (CDBs) when drawing up their integrated local action plans. Arrangements for co-ordination of planning and delivery of services are also to be agreed with the CDBs. Further information on the role of the CDBs is given below, in Section 1.4.

A National Advisory Committee on Drugs (NACD) was established in 1999 by the Cabinet Committee on Social Inclusion, in recognition of the importance of having authoritative information and research findings available to guide policy. The NACD has responsibility for research and information on drug misuse in Ireland. It is implementing a prioritised three-year programme of research and evaluation on the extent, nature, causes and effects of drug misuse in Ireland, and is identifying the contribution to be made by all the relevant interests. The NACD is described in more detail in Moran *et al.* (forthcoming).

1.4   Budget and Funding Arrangements

Given the positive state of the national finances, and the priority the Government has given to the drugs issue, it is not surprising to find that financial allocations in the NDP 2000 – 2006 to address the drugs problem have increased greatly over that allocated in the previous national plan. Accounted for under the broad heading of Social Inclusion, much of the money is being channelled to support local action and community groups in their efforts to tackle the drugs problem. Moreover, where previously, resources were focused on areas where the drugs problem was most acute, with smaller allocations only to other regions, the NDP allocates funds to a number of more geographically-dispersed sub-programmes that address the drugs problem.

Details of funding to support the drugs initiative and Social Inclusion measures are outlined below.

Funding for the drugs area is most appropriately viewed within the context of the Irish Government's NDP, and particularly the NDP's commitment to tackling social exclusion as a policy priority. The NDP covers a seven-year period (2000 – 2006) and involves an investment[3] of Ir£40.588 billion/€51.55 billion of public, EU and private money. The NDP is one element of a nexus of social partnership agreements, which also includes the National Anti-Poverty Strategy (NAPS) and the Programme for Prosperity and Fairness (PPF). Between them they embrace the major sectors and interest groups of civil society and they all address the issue of social inclusion.

The NDP has four broad national objectives:

- continuing sustainable national economic and employment growth;
- consolidating and improving Ireland's international competitiveness;
- fostering regional development; and
- promoting social inclusion.

The NDP comprises three National or Inter-Regional Operational Programmes, as follows:

- Economic and Social Infrastructure;
- Employment and Human Resources;
- Productive Sector;

and two Regional Operational Programmes:

- Border, Midlands and Western (BMW) Region; and
- Southern & Eastern (S&E) Region.

It also contains a separate Operational Programme for the PEACE Programme, which operates in the border counties and Northern Ireland.

Most of the Government's spending in the drugs area is accounted for under the broad objective of Social Inclusion, and is channelled through either National Operational Programmes or the Regional Operational Programmes.

The National Operational Programmes include projects which relate broadly to social inclusion, with important implications for all citizens, including drug misusers – for example, the development of rural transportation will improve access to resources,

---

3   At 1999 prices.

including treatment. This type of 'macro-spending' on social inclusion is complemented by spending under the S&E and BMW Regional Operational Programmes, which are designed to promote, *inter alia*, balanced regional development. The focus at this regional level is on sub-programmes such as Regional Infrastructural Investment, Social Inclusion and Productive Investment. Measures under the Social Inclusion Sub-Programme include Childcare, Equality, Community Development/Family Support, Crime Prevention (many measures here address the drugs area), Youth Services and Services for the Unemployed.

Table 1.1 summarises expenditure on Social Inclusion in the NDP National and Regional Operational Programmes.

TABLE 1.1
Expenditure (€ million) on Social Inclusion, NDP 2000 – 2006.*

Operational Programme	National € million	BMW Region € million	S&E Region € million
Economic and Social Infrastructure	10,157.9	2,451.9	7,706.0
Employment and Human Resources	7,576.7	2,154.7	5,422.0
Regional Programmes/ Social Inclusion	1,343.1	280.1	1,063.00
Total	**19,077.7**	**4,886.7**	**14,191.0**
Expenditure Per Capita	**5,261**	**5,062**	**5,333**

Source : NDP (2000) *Ireland, National Development Plan, 2000 – 2006.*
* In addition to the Community Support Framework there will be four Community Initiative Programmes – Interreg, Equal, Leader and Urban – each supporting some projects in the social inclusion arena.

Under the Regional Operational Programmes, the allocations to combat drug misuse will be IR£112 million/€142 million for the S&E Region, and IR£10 million/€12.7 million for the BMW Region. These funds (IR£122 million/€155 million in total) will be allocated to the LDTFs, and will address the drugs problem under the themes education, prevention, treatment rehabilitation and supply reduction (Department of Tourism, Recreation and Sport, personal communication).

Funding for the LDTFs, and most likely for the YPFSF in 2002, will be channelled through new or adapted structures, which are being or will be put in place to deliver the NDP. Through these structures the implementation of the initiatives will be devolved to the regional level and will involve continued integration of the relevant agencies. Thus, the recently-established CDBs, whose primary function is to draw up a comprehensive Strategy for Economic, Social and Cultural Development by January 2002, have a key role in co-ordinating local delivery of social inclusion measures. The CDBs will operate on the partnership principle, with the Regional Assemblies under the local government umbrella, and with membership drawn from local development organisations, social partners, local representation of State agencies and local government itself (NDP, 2000). A Director of Community and Enterprise has been appointed by each CDB. All the programmes and projects specified by the NDP, and their delivery mechanisms, are to be organised and implemented within this framework.

Key principles underpinning this framework will be (1) the use of common delivery areas, for example, county/city and, where appropriate, local electoral areas for community development/social exclusion, and (2) single agencies being assigned to deliver specific components (e.g. micro-enterprise) of local development in any one area, so as to avoid overlap, confusion and competition between agencies (NDP, 2000).

Preliminary arrangements have been put in place to co-ordinate existing structures involved in the implementation of actions in the drugs area with these new local structures (see Section 1.2 above). Thus, the LDTFs, area-based partnership companies and ADM Community Groups (the local implementing agencies) are due to work with the Directors of Community and Enterprise and the CDBs when drawing up their integrated local action plans. Arrangements for co-ordination of planning and delivery of services are to be agreed with CDBs by the time of the mid-term review of the Regional Operational Programmes in 2003 (Department of Tourism, Recreation and Sport, personal communication).

No detailed breakdowns are available of national expenditure relating to drugs in the areas of law enforcement; epidemiology, prevention and treatment; and evaluation, quality and training; although they were requested by the EMCDDA. The Drug Misuse Research Division's submission to the National Drugs Strategy Review included a recommendation to start work on costing expenditure on drugs; this is also in line with recent EU recommendations, for example, CORDROGUE 64 (1999).

In conclusion, the approach to the drugs problem in Ireland could be described as an integrated, holistic and intersectoral one, which involves the co-ordination of drug programmes and services at local level and focuses on actions to deal with the drugs problem in communities where it is most severe. The forthcoming National Drugs Strategy will frame official analysis of and response to the issue of drugs in Ireland for the immediate future.

1.5 References

Commission of the European Communities (COM) (1999). *Communication from the Commission to the Council and the European Parliament on a European Action Plan to Combat Drugs 2000–2004.* COM (99) 239 Final.

CORDROGUE 64 (1999). *European Union Drug Strategy 2000–2004.* 12555/3/99 REV 3. COREPER document to the Council/European Council.

Department of Health and Children (2000). 'Submission to the National Drugs Strategy Review'. Internal Document. Dublin: The Department of Health and Children.

Drug Misuse Research Division (1999). 'National Report on Drug Issues: Ireland 1999. Report for EMCDDA'. Internal Document. Dublin: Drug Misuse Research Division, The Health Research Board.

Flood, C. (1999). Address by Mr Christopher Flood, at press conference to announce the allocation of funding under the Young People's Facilities and Services Fund in the 13 Local Drug Task Force Areas, Monday 26 April 1999, Dublin. Unpublished.

Inter-Departmental Committee (1998–1999). *Social Inclusion Strategy. National Anti-Poverty Strategy. Annual Report.* Dublin: Stationery Office.

Kelleher, T. (forthcoming). *Perceptions of Use, Availability, and The Responses to Illegal Drugs in Rural Ireland – A study of key informants.* Dublin: Drug Misuse Research Division, The Health Research Board.

Ministerial Task Force on Measures to Reduce the Demand for Drugs (1996). *First Report.* Dublin: Department of the Taoiseach.

Ministerial Task Force on Measures to Reduce the Demand for Drugs (1997). *Second Report.* Dublin: Department of the Taoiseach.

Moran, R., Dillon, L., O'Brien, M., Mayock, P. & Farrell, E. (forthcoming). *A Collection of Papers on Drug Issues in Ireland: Implementation of drug strategy, drug-related infectious diseases, cocaine use and women, children and drug use.* Dublin: Drug Misuse Research Division, The Health Research Board.

NAPS (1998/99; 1999/2000). *National Anti-Poverty Strategy.* Dublin: The Stationery Office.

NDP (2000). *Ireland, National Development Plan 2000 – 2006.* Dublin: The Stationery Office.

O'Brien, M. & Moran, R. (forthcoming). *Drug-Related Knowledge, Attitudes, Beliefs II: Availability, supply, use and location of use – a general population survey.* Dublin: Drug Misuse Research Division, The Health Research Board.

PPF (2000). *Programme for Prosperity and Fairness.* Dublin: The Stationery Office.

CHAPTER 2

LEGAL FRAMEWORK

MARY O'BRIEN, LUCY DILLON AND ROSALYN MORAN

2.1 Introduction

This chapter begins with a brief account in Section 2.2 of the legislation that forms the basis for the control of drugs with a potential for misuse. Section 2.3 comments on the recent changes to drug laws and issues that have arisen in relation to these changes, particularly in relation to health and social matters. A detailed description of the organisation and process involved in the enforcement of drug laws in Ireland is presented in Section 2.4. Finally, Section 2.5 outlines developments in the supply and demand reduction activities/operations of law enforcement agencies.

2.2 Statutes Related to the Control of Drugs with the Potential for Misuse[1]

The following are the Irish laws and regulations, in chronological order, that provide the statutory framework for the control of drugs with a potential for misuse. The legislation is drawn up by relevant government departments: Health and Children; Justice, Equality and Law Reform; and Environment and Local Government. It is implemented by An Garda Síochána (the Irish Police Force), the Revenue Commissioners and the Customs authorities.

---

1 Hard copies of legal texts may be purchased from the Government Publications Sales Office, Sun Alliance House, Molesworth Street, Dublin 2. Electronic versions of the Irish Statute Book (Acts and Statutory Instruments) 1922 – 1998 may be viewed at the website of the Attorney-General's Office www.irlgov.ie/ag/default.htm

Statutes Directly Related to the Control of Drugs

The **Poisons (Ireland) Act, 1870** applies control to the sale of scheduled poisons including opium, morphine, cocaine, heroin and preparations containing these drugs.

The **Pharmacy Act (Ireland), 1875** confines the sale of scheduled substances to authorised persons, i.e. registered pharmaceutical chemists.

The **Probation of Offenders Act, 1907** provides for the majority of non-custodial sanctions available to the courts.

The **Dangerous Drugs Act, 1934**, which was based on international law, controls the import, export, distribution, sale and possession of specified drugs.

The **Medical Preparations (Control of Sale) Regulations, 1966** regulate the retail sale of amphetamines and their analogues, barbiturates and tranquillisers, limiting them to prescription only.

Under the **Medical Preparations (Control of Amphetamines) Regulations, 1969 and 1970** the manufacture, sale and distribution of amphetamines and preparations containing amphetamines or their derivatives are prohibited.

The **Misuse of Drugs Acts, 1977 and 1984**, and the Regulations made thereunder, provide for a wide range of controls over drugs that are liable to misuse. They include controls relating to cultivation, licensing, administration, supply, record keeping, prescription writing, destruction and safe custody. Included in the Acts are provisions designed to deal with the irresponsible prescribing of controlled drugs by medical practitioners (see Table 2.1 for a list of the Acts' associated Regulations).

Possession of any controlled drug, without due authorisation, is an offence under Section 3 of the principal Act (1977). Section 15 of the same Act concerns the possession of a controlled drug for the purpose of unlawful sale or supply. Section 16 details the prohibition of certain activities relating to opium. The use of prepared opium, the frequenting of premises where opium is used and the possession of utensils used for smoking opium are all offences under this section.

The penalties on being found guilty of an offence under Section 15 of the 1977 Act range from a fine or imprisonment for a term not exceeding twelve months, or both, on

TABLE **2.1**
Misuse of Drugs Acts, 1977 and 1984: Act and Regulations in Force
(October 1999).

Misuse of Drugs Act, 1977 (No 12 of 1977)
        (Commencement) Order, 1979 (S.I. No 28 of 1979)
        (Controlled Drugs) (Declaration) Order, 1987 (S.I. No 251 of 1987)
        (Controlled Drugs) (Declaration) Order, 1993 (S.I. No 328 of 1993)

Misuse of Drugs (Licences Fees) Regulations, 1979 (S.I. No 164 of 1979)
        (Amendment) Regulations, 1988 (S.I. No 11 of 1988)

Misuse of Drugs (Custodial Treatment Centre) Order, 1980 (S.I. No 30 of 1980)

Misuse of Drugs (Safe Custody) Regulations, 1982 (S.I. No 321 of 1982)

Misuse of Drugs Act, 1984 (No 18 of 1984)
        (Commencement) Order, 1984 (S.I. No 205 of 1984)

Misuse of Drugs (Committee of Inquiry) Regulations, 1984 (S.I. No 264 of 1984)

Misuse of Drugs (Exemption) Order, 1988 (S.I. No 326 of 1988)
        (Amendment) Order, 1993 (S.I. No 339 of 1993)

Misuse of Drugs Regulations, 1988 (S.I. No 328 of 1988)

Misuse of Drugs (Scheduled Substances) Regulations, 1993 (S.I. No 338 of 1993)
        (Scheduled Substances) (Exemption) Order, 1993 (S.I. No 341 of 1993)
        (Amendment) Regulations, 1993 (S.I. No 342 of 1993)

Misuse of Drugs Regulations (Designation) Order, 1998 (S.I. No 69 of 1998)

Misuse of Drugs (Supervision of Prescription and Supply of Methadone) Regulations, 1998 (S.I. No 225 of 1998)

Misuse of Drugs (Amendment No 1) Regulations, 1999 (S.I. No 273 of 1999)

Customs-Free Airport (Extension of Laws) Regulations, 2000 (S.I. No 169 of 2000)

Source: Department of Health and Children.

summary conviction,[2] to an unlimited fine or imprisonment for life, or both, on conviction on indictment.[3]

The maximum penalty for possession of cannabis for personal use is restricted to a fine for first or second offences tried on summary conviction. For third and subsequent offences there is a fine or twelve months in prison, or both. The penalty for a third offence on indictment is an open-ended fine or three years in prison, or both.

The penalties for the possession of other controlled drugs are harsher and depend on the seriousness of the offence. On summary conviction, the penalty is a fine or twelve months in prison, or both. On conviction on indictment, the maximum fine for possession is left to the discretion of the court, which may impose a seven-year prison sentence, or both a fine and a prison sentence.

Provision is made under the Acts for the judicial possibility in 'certain cases to arrange for the medical or other treatment or for the care' of a person dependent on drugs and convicted of an offence under the Acts.

The **Criminal Justice Act, 1984** provides for a widening of the scope of the criminal law and procedures, to deal more effectively with serious crime, including serious offences under the Misuse of Drugs Acts. Under Section 7, it provides for regulations regarding the treatment of persons in custody in Garda stations. These are covered in the Treatment of Persons in Custody in Garda Síochána Stations Regulations, 1987. If a person in custody is under the influence of drugs and cannot be roused, a doctor must be summoned, or the person must be removed to a hospital or other suitable place if his/her condition necessitates such. Under these regulations a person may also ask to be examined by a doctor of his/her own choice at his/her own expense. The Garda in charge must ensure that any instructions given by a doctor are complied with.

Section 74 of the **Child Care Act, 1991** states that, where a shopkeeper sells a substance, in particular glue, likely to be inhaled to cause intoxication, to a minor, he/she can, on conviction, be fined or imprisoned for up to twelve months. There is a provision for the retailer to put forward a defence that reasonable steps were taken to ensure that this was not a deliberate offence.

---

2   A summary conviction results from a minor offence tried summarily in the District Court before a judge, i.e. without a jury.

3   A conviction on indictment results from a more serious offence tried by a judge and jury at a higher court than the District Court, such as the Circuit Criminal Court.

The **Criminal Justice Act, 1994** provides for the seizure and confiscation of assets derived from the proceeds of drug trafficking and other offences. It contains provisions related to money laundering and allows for international co-operation in respect of certain criminal law enforcement procedures, the forfeiture of property used in the commission of crime, and related matters.

The **Criminal Justice (Drug Trafficking) Act, 1996** provides for the detention of individuals accused of drug trafficking offences for up to seven days. It also allows inferences to be drawn by a court from the failure of an accused person to mention particular facts during questioning.

Under the **Criminal Assets Bureau Act, 1996** the Criminal Assets Bureau (CAB) was established on a statutory footing, with powers to focus on the illegally-acquired assets of criminals involved in serious crime. The aims of the CAB are to identify the criminally-acquired assets of persons and to take appropriate action to deprive such people of these assets. The deprivation is done particularly through the application of the Proceeds of Crime Act, 1996.

The **Licensing (Combating Drug Abuse) Act, 1997** introduces measures allowing for the suspension of intoxicating liquor licences and/or disqualification from ever again obtaining a licence to sell intoxicating liquor, or holding a public dance or a public music and/or singing event, following conviction for drug offences, e.g. knowingly allowing consumption or sale of drugs on premises.

The **Europol Act, 1997** provides for the establishment of a Europol National Unit and enables the ratification, by the State, of the Europol Convention and related protocols. This Convention establishes a European Police Office (Europol) to improve the effectiveness of, and co-operation between, member states in preventing and combating serious international crime involving two or more member states. It provides for a progressive widening of the types of crimes in respect of which Europol will have competence; unlawful drug trafficking offences are included in Europol's initial remit.

Sections 4, 5 and 6 of the **Criminal Justice Act, 1999** make amendments to the Misuse of Drugs Act, 1977, to provide for new drug-related offences. This Act creates a new offence related to the possession of drugs (i.e. an offence under Section 15A of the Misuse of Drugs Act, 1977) with a value of IR£10,000/€12,700 or more, for the purpose of sale or supply. A person found guilty of such an offence may be imprisoned for up to life and be subject to an unlimited fine. The Act also provides for a mandatory minimum sentence of ten years in prison. However, where it is found that addiction was a substantial factor leading to the commission of the offence, the sentence may be reviewed after half the mandatory sentence has been served; at this time the court may suspend the remainder of the sentence on any condition it sees fit.

The **Criminal Justice (Theft and Fraud Offences) Bill, 2000** substitutes a new section for Section 31 of the Criminal Justice Act, 1994, which deals with money laundering. Section 21 of the new Bill makes it an offence for a person to remove the proceeds of criminal activity from the State with the intention of concealing its true nature, or to assist another person to avoid prosecution for criminal offences. The maximum penalty is an unlimited fine or up to fourteen years in prison, or both.[4]

Statutes Indirectly Related to the Control of Drugs

The **Customs Consolidation Act, 1876** is a consolidation of all Customs legislation up to that time and concerns importation, seizures, detention of goods and persons and arrests.

The **Mental Treatment Act, 1945** provides for the compulsory hospitalisation of 'addicts to drugs'. Addiction remains on the statute books as one of the criteria for non-voluntary committal to a psychiatric hospital, but in practice it is not invoked and one of the recommendations of the White Paper on mental health (Department of Health, 1995) was that it be abolished.

The **Customs Act, 1956** 'shall be construed as one with the Customs Acts', which means all enactments relating to the Customs. It deals with the illegal importation and exportation of goods.

The **Customs and Excise (Miscellaneous Provisions) Act, 1988** amends and extends the law relating to customs and duties of excise, and amends the law relating to certain penalties for illicit distillation of spirits. In conjunction with other Customs and Excise legislation, specifically 1876 and 1956, the Customs and Excise (Miscellaneous Provisions) Act, 1988 provides the legal basis for customs controls.

---

4 This is a Bill as distinct from an Act, meaning it has not yet passed into law.

The **Data Protection Act, 1988** is designed to protect the privacy of individuals with regard to automated 'personal data' (data relating to individuals that can be used to identify the individuals). This covers relevant information kept with regard to drug users. The legislation gives effect in Ireland to the Council of Europe Data Protection Convention.

The **Criminal Law (Sexual Offences) Act, 1993**, which mainly deals with the decriminalisation of homosexuality, also includes a number . of clauses covering prostitution. Under this legislation it is an offence to solicit another person for the purpose of prostitution. The penalty on conviction is a fine or three months in prison, or both.

The **Proceeds of Crime Act, 1996** provides for the freezing and forfeiture of the proceeds of crime. This legislation complements the confiscation provisions of the Criminal Justice Act, 1994.

The **Disclosure of Certain Information for Taxation and Other Purposes Act, 1996** provides for more effective exchange of information between An Garda Síochána and the Revenue Commissioners, where there are reasonable grounds for suspecting that profits have been gained from unlawful sources or activities.

The **Children Bill, 1996** is primarily concerned with the introduction of provisions that will allow for the creation and development of a new juvenile justice system. It proposes, for example, that the Garda Juvenile Diversion Programme, which gives the opportunity to divert juvenile offenders from criminal activity and provides an alternative to their being processed through the formal criminal justice system, should operate on a statutory basis. It currently operates on an administrative basis.

The **Freedom of Information Act, 1997** enables members of the public to obtain access to information in the possession of public bodies and to have personal information relating to them corrected.

The **Bail Act, 1997** was enacted to give effect to an amendment to the Constitution, and also to tighten up other areas of the law in relation to the granting of bail. It allows the courts the discretion to refuse bail where they are satisfied that there is a danger that a serious offence will be committed by a person while on bail. The Act also includes a requirement that an accused person and his/her surety lodge in court, in cash or cash equivalent, a proportion of the amount set for bail. It also strengthens the provisions of the Criminal Justice Act, 1984, in relation to the imposition of consecutive sentences for offences committed while on bail.

The **Non-Fatal Offences Against the Person Act, 1997** provides for a range of offences, to combat criminal conduct involving syringes. The Act covers possession of a syringe or container of blood, with intent to threaten or injure; placing or abandoning a syringe in any place in a manner which injures or is likely to injure any person; injuring a person with a syringe or threatening to do so; and throwing or putting blood on another person or threatening to do so. The penalties range from five years to life imprisonment.

The **Housing (Miscellaneous Provisions) Act, 1997** introduces measures designed to assist housing authorities and approved voluntary housing bodies in addressing problems arising on their estates from anti-social behaviour, such as drug dealing. The Act provides for an excluding-order procedure against individual occupants of a local authority house who are involved in anti-social behaviour. This means that the need to evict entire households in certain circumstances can be avoided. It also provides for the Gardaí, on notification by the housing authority, to remove squatters engaged in 'anti-social behaviour' from local authority housing. The Act allows health boards to refuse supplementary welfare allowance, to supplement a person's income in respect of rent or mortgage interest, to individuals who have been prosecuted under the Act.

The **Criminal Justice (Miscellaneous Provisions) Act, 1997** provides for a reduction in the amount of time spent by the Gardaí on court-related duties. This is intended to help ensure a greater uniformed-police presence on the streets. The Act also speeds up aspects of court procedure in criminal matters. It makes general provision, for the first time, for the issue of search warrants in relation to the commission of serious offences, such as murder or rape, and extends the application of certain other Garda powers.

The **Housing (Traveller Accommodation) Act, 1998**, which is the legislative framework within which housing authorities provide for Travellers' accommodation needs, is a key element in the Government's efforts to promote social inclusion and equality and to counter discrimination. This law applies relevant sections of the Housing (Miscellaneous Provisions) Act, 1997 in respect of the control of anti-social behaviour, such as drug dealing, to halting sites provided by local authorities or by voluntary bodies.

2.3 Recent Changes in Legislation and Some Implications

Recent Changes in Legislation

The Misuse of Drugs Acts, 1977 and 1984 provide for a wide range of controls over drugs that have the potential to be misused. They include controls relating to importation, exportation, cultivation, licensing, administration, supply, record keeping, prescription writing, destruction and safe custody. These laws also include provisions designed to deal with the irresponsible prescribing of controlled drugs by medical practitioners. There are a number of exemptions whereby certain categories of people are entitled to possess controlled drugs, for example, Gardaí, Customs officials, or forensic scientists carrying out their duties (Charleton, 1986). The Misuse of Drugs Acts, 1977 and 1984 are the two central pieces of legislation under which the majority of prosecutions in relation to drug misuse are made.

In recent years a number of changes have been made to the legislative framework surrounding drug issues. The Criminal Justice Act, 1999 amends the Misuse of Drugs Act, 1977, to provide for new drug-related offences. This Act creates an offence related to the possession of drugs, with a value of IR£10,000/€12,700 or more, for the purpose of sale or supply. A person found guilty of such an offence may be imprisoned for up to life and may be subject to an unlimited fine. The Act also provides for a mandatory minimum sentence of ten years in prison. However, where it is found that addiction was a substantial factor leading to the commission of the offence, the sentence may be reviewed after half the mandatory sentence has been served; at this time the court may suspend the remainder of the sentence on any condition it sees fit.

The Housing (Traveller Accommodation) Act, 1998, which is the legislative framework within which housing authorities provide for the accommodation needs of Travellers, is a key element in the Government's efforts to promote social inclusion and equality and to counter discrimination. This law applies relevant sections of the Housing (Miscellaneous Provisions) Act, 1997, dealing with anti-social behaviour, such as drug dealing, to halting sites provided by local authorities or by voluntary bodies.

New legislation in relation to mental health, which is currently being drawn up, proposes that addiction will be excluded from the scope of the legal definition of mental disorder. Although, in practice, it is not invoked, under current legislation (the Mental Treatment Act, 1945), addiction remains on the statute books as a criterion for non-voluntary committal to a psychiatric hospital. It is now considered unacceptable to detain, by law, people whose primary problem is addiction.

New regulations introduced in 1999 (Misuse of Drugs (Amendment No 1) Regulations, 1999) give authority to certain officials in the Department of Agriculture to possess cannabis hemp, lawfully, as part of their duties in monitoring and sampling in the production of hemp fibre.

In 2000 new regulations (Customs-Free Airport (Extension of Laws) Regulations, 2000) were introduced to extend drug controls under the Misuse of Drugs Acts, 1977 and 1984, and the Irish Medicines Board Act, 1995, to include the Customs-free area at Shannon Airport. This instrument covers a loophole in the legislation and allows the Irish Medicines Board to inspect any company within the Customs-free area at Shannon Airport.

An order has been drafted (Misuse of Drugs Act, 1977 (Controlled Drugs) (Declaration) Order, 1999) to extend the list of substances controlled under the Misuse of Drugs Acts. The need to do this arose out of Ireland's obligations under the UN Conventions on Narcotic Drugs, Psychotropic Substances and Precursor Chemicals,[5] and also because of concerns about the abuse of amphetamine-type substances, and the use of certain drugs in sport. The drugs to be controlled include substances associated with ecstasy misuse (4-MTA, ketamine, ephedrine and pseudoephedrine), and substances on the current International Olympics Committee's list of prohibited substances in an effort to prevent doping in sport. This order will come into force in 2001.

Some Health and Social Implications

Some health and social implications have arisen, particularly in relation to the implementation of two pieces of legislation. The first is a health issue arising from the Criminal Law (Sexual Offences) Act, 1993. A study carried out by the Women's Health Project in Dublin (O'Neill & O'Connor, 1999) found that the legislation dealing with prostitution was having a negative impact on the lives of prostitutes. The researchers commented that an increasing number of complaints from local residents, and a requirement in the legislation that anyone 'loitering for the purposes of prostitution' be directed from the area, had resulted in sex workers' going underground and working in increasingly unsafe environments. Consequently, it was becoming more difficult for health workers, aiming to provide healthcare and prevent the spread of HIV, to reach the women. This was seen to have serious implications for public health policy. The authors of the study recommended that a review of the current legislation be undertaken as soon as possible.

The second implication is both a social and a health issue and relates to housing legislation (Housing (Miscellaneous Provisions) Act, 1997) and its effect on drug users. This law allows public housing authorities to initiate an excluding-order procedure against occupants of local authority housing who are 'involved in anti-social behaviour'.

---

5   The conventions may be accessed through the website – www.incb.org/e/conv/

A study of the impact of the legislation (Memery & Kerrins, 2000) found that it gave local authorities the legal go-ahead to evict tenants and to use indirect means, such as encouraging other family members to exclude the individual, in order to remove those considered to be involved in anti-social behaviour, much of which was drug related. People excluded from access to public housing can find themselves also discriminated against in seeking hostel accommodation because of their drug use.

The exclusion of the individual involved in anti-social behaviour from the home results in the loss of essential family supports, as well as removal from community-based drug services. The report stated that 'street homelessness resulting from exclusion leads to open drug taking and riskier drug taking practices' (Memery *et al.*, 2000: 33). Such behaviour will increase the risk of contracting infectious diseases. A study of out-of-home drug users (Cox & Lawless, 1999) suggested that the housing legislation had contributed to the rise in homelessness among drug users (see also Section 5.2). It should be noted, however, that this legislation is warmly welcomed by certain community groups and activists and is seen as a means to protect quality of life on housing estates where serious drug problems exist.

Other aspects of drug legislation were criticised at the public National Crime Forum, held in 1998. One issue was the provision under the Criminal Justice (Drug Trafficking) Act, 1996, that allows the Gardaí to detain a person accused of drug trafficking for a period of seven days. Some contributors to the Forum considered that this provision could prove to be counterproductive, resulting in more convictions of drug users and small-time dealers rather than curbing the activities of large-scale drug traffickers (National Crime Forum, 1998). Another was the proposal (now incorporated in the Criminal Justice Act, 1999) to provide for a new drug offence relating to the possession of drugs, with a value of IR£10,000/€12,700 or more, for the purpose of sale or supply, and for a mandatory minimum sentence of ten years in prison. It was criticised 'both on grounds of principle relating to mandatory sentences generally and because of the difficulty of establishing the actual value of a seizure' (National Crime Forum, 1998: 72).

2.4 Drug Law Enforcement Organisation and Process

This section describes the organisation and process to enforce drug laws in Ireland. Two main areas are covered:

• Drug Law Enforcement Organisation
• Drug Law Enforcement Process

FIGURE 2.1
Drug Law Enforcement Organisation

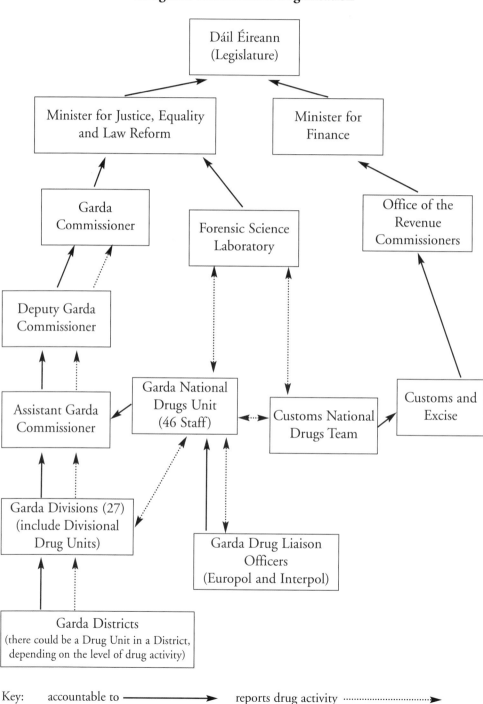

Key: accountable to ⟶   reports drug activity ┈┈┈▶

Drug Law Enforcement Organisation

This section examines how the enforcement agencies are organised and the relationships between the various agencies (see Figure 2.1).

An Garda Síochána is the national police force in Ireland. It has responsibility for the State security services and all traffic and criminal law enforcement functions, including those laws related to drug offences.[6]

The general management and control of An Garda Síochána is the responsibility of the Garda Commissioner, who is appointed by the Government. He or she is responsible to the Minister for Justice, Equality and Law Reform, who in turn is accountable to Dáil Éireann (the Irish legislature) for the activities of the force. The Commissioner carries out his/her duties within the constraints of regulations laid down by the Minister for Justice, Equality and Law Reform. In addition to the Commissioner, there are two Deputy Commissioners and nine Assistant Commissioners.

In descending order, the ranking of officers in An Garda Síochána is as follows:

• Commissioner
• Deputy Commissioner
• Assistant Commissioner
• Chief Superintendent
• Superintendent
• Inspector
• Sergeant
• Garda

Ireland is divided into twenty-seven Divisions for policing purposes, each of which is commanded by a Chief Superintendent. The Dublin Metropolitan Region is made up of six Divisions, which are operated as a unit, commanded by an Assistant Commissioner. Each Division is divided into Districts, which are commanded by a Superintendent, assisted by one or more Inspectors as appropriate. These Districts are further divided into Sub-Districts, each normally the responsibility of a Sergeant. Each Sub-District usually only has one station, the personnel strength of which will vary from 3 to 100. In some areas there are stations known as sub-stations (usually 'one-officer' stations), which, for administrative purposes, are attached to a parent station. In total, there are approximately 700 Garda stations nationally.

---

6   The following organisational information on An Garda Síochána may be found on their website: www.irlgov.ie/garda/

As part of their training, all Irish Gardaí receive instruction in the area of drug misuse. The programme includes training in:

- the enforcement of drug-related laws;
- the procedures for dealing with drug cases; and
- health and safety issues.

Special units have been integrated into the organisational structure of An Garda Síochána in an effort to address the drugs issue. In each of the country's twenty-seven Garda Divisions, there is a specialised Drug Unit, which has responsibility for the enforcement of drugs legislation. There may also be a Drug Unit in a District where drugs present particular problems. The staff size of each Drug Unit will depend on the level of drug activity in the area, but typically a Drug Unit comprises a Sergeant and between one and eight Gardaí (Garda National Drugs Unit, personal communication).

The **Garda National Drugs Unit (GNDU)** was established in 1995 with specific responsibility for drug law enforcement. There are currently forty-six personnel working in the GNDU (including a Customs liaison officer), and the Unit is headed by a Detective Chief Superintendent, who reports to the Assistant Commissioner for Crime, Security and Traffic. The primary focus of the GNDU is to target major drug traffickers, as well as monitoring, controlling and evaluating all 'drug' intelligence and policies within the force (An Garda Síochána, 1995). As part of its focus on the national and international aspects of drug trafficking, the GNDU maintains close liaison with police forces from other jurisdictions, through various police networks and operational exchange programmes (An Garda Síochána, 1999a). Another function of the GNDU is to provide support, through training, joint operations and advice, for the Divisional Drug Units described above (An Garda Síochána, 1999a).

The **Forensic Science Laboratory** of the Department of Justice, Equality and Law Reform is responsible for the analysis (including the type and purity) of illicit drugs seized by law enforcement agencies and the collection of seizure statistics. The laboratory is also involved in the development of analytical techniques for the identification of illicit substances.

The **Office of the Revenue Commissioners** is an organisation separate from the Department of Finance, but within the area of responsibility of the Minister for Finance, and includes the **Customs and Excise Service**. Customs have primary responsibility for the prevention, detection, interception and seizure of controlled drugs, intended to be smuggled or imported illegally into the State.

The **Customs National Drugs Team** was established in December 1992. The principal role of the Team is to direct the work of Customs on the prevention of drugs smuggling and the enforcement of legislative provisions regarding the import and export of controlled drugs and other substances. The Team has over seventy personnel, who are assigned to Intelligence, Operational, Maritime and Dog Handler Units (Office of the Revenue Commissioners, 1994). These units are strategically located around the coast of Ireland in an effort to prevent drug trafficking (Office of the Revenue Commissioners, 1993).

Under the Customs and Excise (Miscellaneous Provisions) Act, 1988, members of the Customs Service may arrest a suspect at the point of entry into the country. However, the investigation of an offence is the responsibility of An Garda Síochána. Interagency co-operation has increased between the two agencies and a memorandum of understanding and a working protocol have been drawn up. To facilitate interagency co-operation, An Garda Síochána have a liaison officer with the Customs Service and a Customs liaison officer is based at the GNDU (An Garda Síochána, 1999a).

Drug Law Enforcement Process

The following description of the process involved in drug law enforcement starts from the first point of intervention by a member of An Garda Síochána through to sentencing procedures (see Figure 2.2).

Intervention – At the point of intervention a suspect can be detained either by a member of An Garda Síochána or a Customs official. The Customs Service has responsibility for the detection of the illegal importation of illicit substances at the point of entry into the country. Any offence arising therefrom, or within the State (as distinct from the point of entry), is the responsibility of An Garda Síochána.

Arrest/Detention, Investigation and Charge – When a drug trafficking incident is reported, or an offence detected, a person can be detained by the Gardaí without being charged, subject to judicial approval, for up to seven days under the Criminal Justice (Drug Trafficking) Act, 1996. For a less serious offence (including other drug-related offences), a person can be detained for twelve hours under the Criminal Justice Act, 1984. After an initial six-hour period, approval to detain an individual for a further six hours must be sought from the relevant Garda Superintendent. After the total twelve-hour period, a person must either be charged with an offence[7] or released without charge.

---

7   This is the point at which proceedings commence and data are routinely collected and published each year.

FIGURE 2.2
Drug Law Enforcement Process

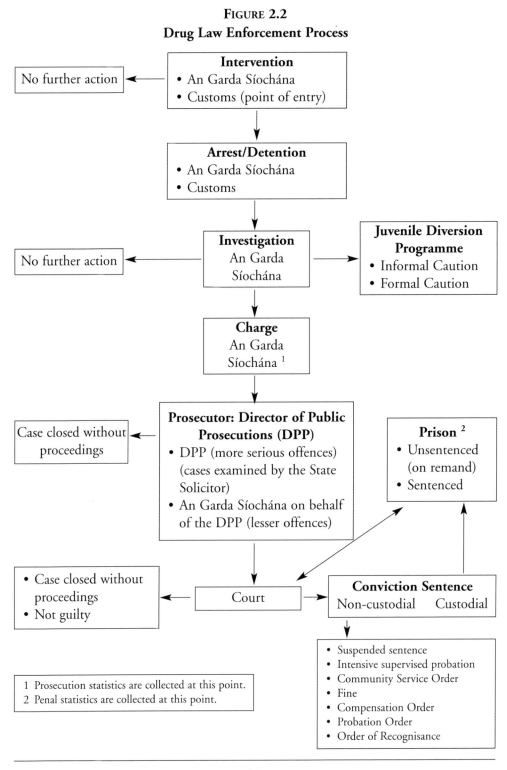

Intervention
- An Garda Síochána
- Customs (point of entry)

No further action

Arrest/Detention
- An Garda Síochána
- Customs

Investigation
An Garda Síochána

No further action

Juvenile Diversion Programme
- Informal Caution
- Formal Caution

Charge
An Garda Síochána [1]

Prosecutor: Director of Public Prosecutions (DPP)
- DPP (more serious offences) (cases examined by the State Solicitor)
- An Garda Síochána on behalf of the DPP (lesser offences)

Case closed without proceedings

Prison [2]
- Unsentenced (on remand)
- Sentenced

- Case closed without proceedings
- Not guilty

Court

Conviction Sentence
Non-custodial   Custodial

- Suspended sentence
- Intensive supervised probation
- Community Service Order
- Fine
- Compensation Order
- Probation Order
- Order of Recognisance

1 Prosecution statistics are collected at this point.
2 Penal statistics are collected at this point.

No programmes are in place at this point in the process, providing treatment/care for addicted persons entering the judicial system. Furthermore, where drugs are involved, the Gardaí have no discretionary powers to issue a caution (informal or formal) or to impose an on-the-spot fine. An exception is made in the case of a juvenile offender (under 18 years old) found in possession of a small amount of drugs, where drug trafficking is not an issue. In such a case, the Garda Juvenile Diversion Programme is brought to bear. This programme was introduced in 1963 with the aim of diverting juvenile offenders from criminal activity. The programme allows that, if certain criteria are met, a juvenile offender may be cautioned as an alternative to being prosecuted (An Garda Síochána, 1999b). The programme operates on the basis of the common law principle of police discretion.

While the Garda Juvenile Diversion Programme is specifically aimed at juvenile offenders committing first offences, it may be adapted/extended to include juveniles committing subsequent offences. A juvenile offender who is eligible for inclusion in the programme is dealt with by way of a caution, as opposed to being prosecuted for a criminal offence. Cautions may be either formal or informal. A Juvenile Liaison Officer (JLO) becomes involved with the offender and the family. While an informal caution may be given by the JLO, a formal caution must be given by the Garda Superintendent of the District where the offender lives. There is no provision for a similar system of cautioning for adults.

Prosecution – The Irish system of criminal prosecution is an accusatorial and adversarial system, developed from the common law, in which the onus of proving guilt beyond a reasonable doubt rests on the prosecutor. All criminal prosecutions in Ireland are taken under the authority of the Director of Public Prosecutions (DPP).

In practice, the DPP gives blanket authority to An Garda Síochána to prosecute lesser offences.[8] The seriousness of an offence is determined by a number of factors, e.g. the value of the drugs involved, whether it is a trafficking offence. In these cases it is the function of the Gardaí, not alone to investigate the crime, but also to initiate prosecutions and, in summary cases,[9] to prosecute offenders to verdict. The vast majority of criminal prosecutions are prosecuted summarily and are initiated and prosecuted by An Garda Síochána in the District Court, without any direct involvement of the DPP in the process. The prosecution is usually made by the member of An Garda Síochána who investigated the matter, under the name of the DPP (Office of the Director of Public Prosecutions, 1999).

---

8   This practice has been identified as almost unique to the Irish system (Office of the Director of Public Prosecutions, 1999).
9   A summary case deals with a minor offence, triable summarily before a judge, i.e. without a jury.

In more serious cases, a file outlining the case must be sent to the DPP by the Gardaí. All files sent to the DPP go to the State Solicitor. The State Solicitor acts as a conduit by examining the legal aspects of the charge and making a recommendation as to whether the DPP should proceed with a prosecution or not. A decision may be made at this stage to close the case without further proceedings.

The defendant is either served with a summons to appear before the District Court on a certain date, or else he/she may be arrested, following which he/she must be brought to the District Court for formal charging within hours of arrest. Therefore, the two distinct methods by which a defendant is brought before the court are by means of either a summons or a charge sheet. The defendant usually seeks legal aid at his/her first court appearance and, if granted, a solicitor is appointed to represent him/her. The solicitor may then apply for access to statements made by the witnesses and copies of any forensic reports made, access to which is usually granted by the court. The onus of proving guilt always rests on the prosecution.

No programmes are in place to provide treatment/care for addicted persons at this stage of the judicial system.

Court – The Courts in Ireland were established under the provisions of the Constitution of Ireland. The Constitution of Ireland provides that 'justice shall be administered in public in courts established by law, and by judges appointed by the President on the advice of the Government' (Courts Service, website www.courts.ie).

In drug cases, the DPP must consent to summary trial. In other words, the DPP picks the forum for trial. This is the practice in relation to most offences under modern statutes. Where offences come under older legislation, including the statute for offences of larceny (1916), the defendant always has the right to elect to be tried summarily in the District Court or on indictment before a judge and jury in the Circuit Court.[10] The right to choose trial before a judge and jury, therefore, is not usually available to a defendant on a drugs charge, as the Misuse of Drugs Acts are modern statutes. In these cases only the DPP can select the forum for trial.

The decision made on the forum for trial will depend on the gravity of the charge – for example, in the case of a drug seizure, on the quantity and value of the drugs involved. A distinction is made between indictable and non-indictable offences (summary offences). Some indictable offences may be disposed of summarily in the District Court.

---

10 A trial on indictment deals with a more serious offence, triable by a judge and jury at a higher court than the District Court, such as the Circuit Criminal Court.

In other cases, the DPP may direct that an indictable offence be heard without a jury at the Special Criminal Court, which was set up under Part V of the Offences Against the State Act, 1939, to deal with terrorist offences, and at which three judges preside. The two courts within the Irish system at which drug offenders or offenders who are misusing drugs generally present – the District Court and the Circuit Criminal Court – are described below.

The **District Court** is a court of first instance, that is, all prosecutions for criminal offences begin in the District Court, irrespective of whether they proceed to a higher court such as the Circuit Criminal Court, Central Criminal Court or Special Criminal Court. Indictable offences, which are not dealt with in the District Court, proceed to the Circuit Criminal Court (or the High Court), but only after a preliminary examination in the District Court. As such, the District Court deals with summary offences and indictable offences triable summarily. In practice, the vast majority of indictable offences are disposed of summarily in the District Court. The offences dealt with by the District Court include drug offences and larceny.

Before an offence is triable in the District Court, the District Court judge must accept the offence as being a minor case capable of being tried summarily; in other words, the District Court judge must decide that the likely penalty will not exceed the penalty jurisdiction of the District Court. The District Court can impose a fine, one of a range of non-custodial sanctions or a prison sentence. The maximum permitted prison sentences are twelve months for a single offence, and twenty-four months for consecutive sentences.

The **Circuit Criminal Court** also deals with drug offences. This court may try any indictable offence, with the exception of treason, murder, attempted murder, conspiracy to commit murder, piracy, rape, aggravated sexual assault and attempted aggravated sexual assault. An indictable offence is more serious than a summary offence. The offence is chargeable by way of a bill of indictment, accompanied by the book of evidence, the defendant having been returned for trial by the District Court judge either from custody or on bail. For indictable offences, the defendant is entitled to a trial by jury.

The preliminary examination procedure is provided for in the Criminal Procedure Act, 1967. A book of evidence is served on the defendant, and contains a statement of the charges and a statement of the evidence. Before the defendant can be sent forward for trial on indictment before a judge and jury, the District Court judge must be satisfied, having read the book of evidence and having heard any depositions, that a *prima facie* case is disclosed. In practice, drug-related crimes considered by the DPP to be too serious, are tried in the Circuit Criminal Court. Similarly, appeal cases from the District Court are heard in the Circuit Criminal Court.

Conviction Sentence – In addition to custodial measures, there is a range of non-custodial options available to sentence those who plead guilty or are found guilty through the Courts. The decision of the court in relation to the imposition of a custodial or non-custodial sentence may be influenced by a Pre-Sanction Report, where available. This report is compiled by the Probation and Welfare Services, and includes information on factors, such as addiction, that may have contributed to the individual's offending. However, Pre-Sanction Reports are often not available, although a judge may request that one be provided.

The non-custodial options available to the courts in relation to drug convictions include a range of options, listed below.[11]

A **Suspended Sentence**[12] applies when a convicted defendant is sentenced to a period of imprisonment by a court, but part or all of the sentence is suspended, on condition that the defendant enters into a bond to be of good behaviour and not re-offend for the period of time as set by the court. Effectively, the convicted defendant is 'on bail' for the remainder of the sentence.

Supervision during Deferment of Penalty[13]**/ Intensive Supervised Probation** was designed to increase restraints on offenders in the community. Offenders are required to report for frequent urine testing. The type and level of demand placed on offenders differ enormously by jurisdiction.

A **Community Service Order** requires offenders to perform unpaid work for between 40 and 240 hours. It has been suggested by the Probation and Welfare Services that within the Courts system there is a perceived lack of suitable community service for offenders with addiction (Expert Group on the Welfare and Probation Services, 1999).

A **Fine** has statutory limits, fixed for a particular offence. The money is paid to Central Funds (a fund administered by the Department of Justice, Equality and Law Reform), and if unpaid can be enforced by committal to prison.

---

11 An overview of non-custodial options was given in a report on the Irish Probation and Welfare Services (Expert Group on the Probation and Welfare Services, 1999).
12 This option has no statutory basis but is widely used by the Courts.
13 This option has no statutory basis but is widely used by the Courts.

A **Compensation Order** has a specific statutory format, laid out in the Criminal Justice Act, 1993, and is related to the wrong done. The money goes to the victim as opposed to Central Funds.

A **Fine and Compensation Order** requires the offender to pay both a fine and compensation under the two preceding penalties.

A **Release under the Probation of Offenders Act, 1907** means that a decision is made not to proceed to convict.

The purpose of a **Probation Order under Probation of Offenders Act, 1907,** is to secure the rehabilitation of the offender, to protect the public and to prevent the offender from committing further offences. This is used for drug users by imposing conditions. Conditions may include attendance for treatment and the provision of urine for analysis. This is the preferred procedure in the District Court when dealing with drug users.

An **Order of Recognisance (Misuse of Drugs Act, 1977, Section 28, as amended by the Misuse of Drugs Act, 1984)** requires an offender to undergo treatment for his/her drug condition in a residential centre or in the community. The Order of Recognisance would appear to be an important non-custodial option for drug users who offend in Ireland. However, in practice, the Courts do not generally use this order. The necessary rules and regulations have not been made. Furthermore, the provision of a statutory place of treatment has always been problematic. The Expert Group on the Probation and Welfare Services has recommended that the necessary Courts Rules and Regulations be updated by the various Court Rules Committees to facilitate wider use of the Order of Recognisance (Expert Group on the Probation and Welfare Services, 1999).

While the legislative framework (the Order of Recognisance (Misuse of Drugs Act, 1977, Section 28, as amended by the Misuse of Drugs Act, 1984)) exists for the non-custodial option of requiring an individual to undergo treatment for drug addiction, in practice it is imposed rarely by the Courts. The establishment of a **Drug Courts** system, initially on a pilot basis in Dublin, under the jurisdiction of the District Court, is planned for January 2001. These courts are intended to be treatment oriented, where people with a drug problem, who are charged with non-violent offences, are diverted to treatment programmes rather than to prison. This development is likely to have major implications for treatment services and the success of the initiative will depend on the formulation and implementation of cohesive treatment and rehabilitation programmes.

2.5 Activities Relating to Supply and Demand Reduction

Up to the mid-1990s Garda activity focused mainly on supply reduction and law enforcement. Since 1995, however, the area of demand reduction has become a more important and prominent aspect of policing the drug problem. The fostering of strong community links is seen as an important aspect of effective policing. The following is a summary of developments that have taken place in recent years.

Institutional Developments

A **Garda National Drugs Unit (GNDU)** was established in September 1995, replacing the former Dublin-based Drug Squad. The establishment of the GNDU was a marked departure in that it placed responsibility for drug law enforcement at a national level. It also introduced the concept of demand reduction to Garda activities.

'Policing In Ireland', the new five-year corporate strategy for An Garda Síochána, was put in place on 1 January 2000. The enforcement of laws relating to drugs was one of the major priorities identified. Operationally this will involve each manager in each Garda Division/District and Station drawing up specific plans/targets, reviewing progress and adjusting strategy as needed (Sutton, 2000).

Each of the twenty-seven Garda Divisions in the country has a specialised **Drug Unit** with responsibility for enforcement of drugs legislation. In the cities of Dublin, Limerick and Cork, Districts have Drug Units as well, dealing with the drug problem at local level. For example, since January 2000 there have been eighteen dedicated Drug Units in the Dublin Metropolitan Region. They are in constant liaison with each other and with the GNDU (Sutton, 2000).

The Garda Commissioner is represented on the **National Drugs Strategy Team** by a Detective Superintendent from GNDU.

Each of the **Local Drug Task Forces (LDTFs)** has a Garda representative at Inspector level.

Community Policing Forums have been set up to allow the Gardaí to work with local community groups and individuals in targeting drug pushers, as well as improving overall relations between the Gardaí and local communities. A number of these are being supported by LDTFs. A 'policing forum' is being piloted in south inner-city Dublin.

Legislation is being prepared to establish the **Irish Prisons Service** as an independent statutory service. The first Director-General was appointed on 15 July 1999 and given responsibility for day-to-day management of the prison system. Among the Director-General's priorities is the provision of medical care to prisoners on a par with public health care in the community. To this end, two major initiatives have been taken. Firstly, the Irish Prisons Service in July 2000 published the *First Report of the Steering Group on Prison Based Drug Treatment Services* (Irish Prisons Service, 2000). This report identifies the resources required, at individual prison level, to put in place a systematic approach to treatment of prisoners with drug dependencies. The report indicated that the Eastern Regional Health Authority (ERHA) would have substantial input into the delivery of drug treatment. On foot of this report, the Government (18 October 2000) approved the new approach to drug treatment in prisons. It is estimated by the Director-General that full implementation of the programme will take at least two years, involving recruitment and training of staff and key professionals, *inter alia*. Secondly, a group has been established to conduct a comprehensive review of the structure and organisation of prison healthcare services. This group's report is due for publication in the middle of 2001.

The Department of Justice, Equality and Law Reform's discussion paper '**Tackling Crime**' (Department of Justice, Equality and Law Reform, 1997) stated that the link between crime and disadvantage was real. In order to widen the debate on crime and its causes, a **National Crime Forum** was established; it reported in 1998 (National Crime Forum, 1998). Following publication of the report, the Minister established the **National Crime Council** in 1999. The Council is established on an initial two-year non-statutory basis. The establishment of the Council is intended to facilitate broadly-based and well-informed discussion on crime on an ongoing basis and will serve as an important aid to policy formulation. The key roles envisaged for the council are to (1) focus on crime prevention, with particular emphasis on the underlying causes of crime and the development of partnerships and practical approaches which will be effective at community level; (2) focus directly on raising public knowledge and awareness of crime; (3) examine the 'fear of crime' and address the issues, including those relating to minorities, which arise as a consequence of this fear; and (4) identify research priorities, which could be commissioned by the Department of Justice, Equality and Law Reform.

A **White Paper on Crime** will be prepared in 2001. This paper will focus on linkages between the various agencies within the system, and in the wider sense between the causes of crime and the Government's specific measures to target social inclusion.

Interagency co-operation has increased and is seen as vital in combating the international drug trade. Accordingly, there is growing co-operation between An Garda

Síochána, the Customs Service and the Naval Service. A memorandum of understanding and a working protocol have been drawn up between An Garda Síochána and the Customs Service. Both agencies engage in joint training programmes and exercises with the Naval Service. The interagency co-operation involved in the operation of the Criminal Assets Bureau (CAB), including the Gardaí, the Department of Social, Community and Family Affairs, and the Revenue Commissioners, has been very successful in the freezing and forfeiture of the proceeds of criminal activity, including drug-related crime.

International Developments

EU and international co-operation has also increased greatly since 1995. Drug Liaison Officers have been established in The Hague, Europol and Madrid. In June 1998 a Drug Liaison Officer was posted to Interpol, Lyons, on a permanent basis.

An EU-funded initiative, the **Oisín Programme**, was adopted by the Council of Ministers in 1996. The aim is to improve channels of communication, to identify international drug dealers, to share information and best practice in relation to demand reduction, training and intelligence gathering, and to exchange insights in relation to the working methods of participating police forces. Police forces in Ireland, Finland, Northern Ireland, Portugal, Scotland and Wales are collaborating in an initiative to examine the extent and effects of controlled drugs in rural areas, and to formulate programmes to counteract the threat posed. A new Oisín Programme started in 2000.

Within the EU, An Garda Síochána is represented at senior management level in the following working groups – the Horizontal Drugs Working Group, the Police Co-operation Working Group, the Multi-disciplinary Group, the EU Working Party on Drug Trafficking and the Mixed Committee on Drug Trafficking.

National/Regional Initiatives

Ireland has the strongest legislation in Europe for countering drugs. The **Criminal Justice (Drug Trafficking) Act, 1996** allows for seven days' detention of a suspect without charge. This is subject to the approval of senior Gardaí for the first forty-eight hours (for three periods – six hours, eighteen hours, twenty-four hours), and then judicial approval for subsequent detainment(s) (seventy-two hours and forty-eight hours), when the suspect must be brought to Court before a judge. Under the **Proceeds of Crime Act, 1996** the onus is on the person suspected of a crime to prove that assets were obtained legitimately.

A **Coastal Watch Programme** has been established where local people assist in policing Ireland's 3,000 miles of coastline. Each coastal division is assigned an Inspector with specific responsibility for liaison with the local community so as to channel information and intelligence more effectively.

Complaints by communities regarding open drug dealing on the streets led to the setting up of **Operation Cleanstreet** – an undercover operation to identify small-time drug dealers. Initially, the Operation focused on a few areas in Dublin where open dealing had become a major problem, but it is now a nation-wide initiative and has included operations in Kells, Navan, Trim and Drogheda. Five Operation Cleanstreet programmes have been put in place and over 500 street dealers have been identified / prosecuted.

Garda presence at large music events, for example Homelands in Mosney and Creamfields in Punchestown, has increased, along with arrests of persons found in possession of controlled drugs or in possession for the purpose of supply.

Operation Nightcap, designed to target licensed premises that allow the consumption, sale and supply of controlled drugs from the premises, has been implemented.

Operation Rectify, designed to target individuals involved in the sale and supply of controlled drugs and prescription drugs in the vicinity of treatment centres, is under way.

Operation Tap, designed to target individuals engaged in the sale and supply of controlled drugs to the homeless and prostitutes, particularly in central Dublin, has been introduced.

Operation Dochas, designed to make substantial inroads into the drug problem in Dublin, through the identification of the critical areas requiring action and the deployment of Gardaí solely to this operation in these communities, has been established.

Drug Courts are planned on a pilot basis in Dublin for January 2001. Commentators stress that development of the necessary supportive infrastructure is a prerequisite to the success of the initiative. An independent evaluation of the pilot is planned.

The Department of Justice, Equality and Law Reform is involved in a number of initiatives in the area of '**diversion**'. Intensive probation supervision is provided through a number of projects. These projects divert serious offenders from prison at the court stage, and place them in a community-based programme, with the ultimate aim of reintegrating them into employment. The EU INTEGRA programme funds the **CONNECT** project, which aims to reintegrate certain prisoners (in Mountjoy Prison), some of whom may have had drug addiction problems, into society and the workforce. A further phase of the project was implemented in November 2000.

The Garda Community Relations Section has established a number of crime prevention and intervention programmes throughout the country, known as **Garda Youth Diversion Projects**. These projects are funded by the Department of Justice, Equality and Law Reform and are generally managed by Foróige and/or the City of Dublin Youth Service Board. At present there are thirty-nine projects throughout the country, ten of which were established as part of the first phase of the expansion of the Garda Juvenile Diversion Programme under the National Development Plan (NDP) in 2000. An additional IR£16 million / €20,316 has been provided over the life of the NDP to facilitate a significant expansion of this particular programme. Provision for further phases of this expansion is well advanced.

2.6 References

Charleton, P. (1986). *Controlled Drugs and the Criminal Law*. Dublin: An Clo Liuir, 10 Salzburg, Ardilea, Dublin 14.

Cox, G. & Lawless, M. (1999). *Wherever I Lay My Hat… A Study of Out of Home Drug Users*. Dublin: Merchant's Quay Project.

Department of Health (1995). *White Paper. A new mental health act*. Dublin: The Stationery Office.

Department of Justice, Equality and Law Reform (1997). *Tackling Crime*. Dublin: The Stationery Office.

Expert Group on the Probation and Welfare Services (1999). *Final Report of the Expert Group on the Probation and Welfare Services*. Dublin: The Stationery Office.

An Garda Síochána (1995). *Annual Report of An Garda Síochána 1995*. Dublin: The Stationery Office.

An Garda Síochána (1999a). *Annual Report of An Garda Síochána 1998*. Dublin: The Stationery Office.

An Garda Síochána (1999b). *Annual Report of An Garda Síochána 1999*. Dublin: The Stationery Office.

Irish Prisons Service (2000). *Report of the Steering Group on Prison Based Drug Treatment Services*. Dublin: Irish Prisons Service.

Memery, C. & Kerrins, L. (2000). *Estate Management and Anti-Social Behaviour in Dublin. A study of the impact of the Housing (Miscellaneous Provisions) Act 1997*. Dublin: Threshold.

National Crime Forum (1998). *Report of the National Crime Forum 1998*. Dublin: Institute of Public Administration.

Office of the Director of Public Prosecutions (1999). *Office of the Director of Public Prosecutions Annual Report 1998*. Dublin: Office of the Director of Public Prosecutions.

Office of the Revenue Commissioners (1993). *The Revenue Commissioners Annual Report 1992*. Dublin: The Stationery Office.

Office of the Revenue Commissioners (1994). *The Revenue Commissioners Annual Report 1993*. Dublin: The Stationery Office.

O'Neill, M. & O'Connor, A. M. (1999). *Drug-using Women Working in Prostitution*. Dublin: The Women's Health Project, Eastern Health Board.

Sutton, B. (2000). 'An Overview of Supply Reduction Measures in Operation at Local Level'. Paper presented at public meeting at Marino Institute, Dublin, to document public representations to the Review of the National Drugs Strategy. Unpublished.

CHAPTER 3

RESEARCH FINDINGS ON DRUG USE

MARY O'BRIEN

3.1 Introduction

Historically there has been little survey research carried out in Ireland on drug use among adults in the general population. The first nation-wide survey of drug use among adults was carried out by the Centre for Health Promotion Studies, National University of Ireland (NUI), Galway in 1998, as part of a large Survey of Lifestyle, Attitudes and Nutrition (SLÁN). The findings of the drug use module of this survey have not yet been published but statistics have been made available to the Drug Misuse Research Division (DMRD) of the Health Research Board (HRB).

Information on drug use among school pupils is more readily available. However, most of the studies have been conducted at regional level and have differed in terms of methodology, sample size, questionnaire design, and age groups surveyed. In addition, differences in theoretical approaches (health behaviours, health promotion, education/ prevention, problem drug-use behaviours), reflecting different perspectives, can preclude meaningful comparisons of survey results.

The lifetime experience of drug use (that is, respondents reporting that they have used at some time in the past) among young people in Ireland is widespread, but this does not necessarily mean that they continue to use drugs after an initial experience, or go on to become regular users. A sizeable minority of young people have tried cannabis at some time in their lives. Media reports tend to concentrate on such figures, without any reference to what is meant by lifetime experience. Drug use in the past year or the past month is more informative about recent use, but distinctions about timescales tend to be ignored in media reports on drug use. Recent use tends to be considerably less than lifetime use, and an increase in lifetime use does not necessarily mean that there is also an increase in recent use.

Several factors, including the media, can influence society's perceptions of drug use and drug users, and research evidence may sometimes be at variance with what is perceived by society as a whole. When discussing drug issues, 'It is important to look beyond the stereotypes or reliance on the media-fed explanations of phenomena' (Nic Gabhainn & Walsh, 2000: 2).

The authors of a study on the attitudes of the general public to drug use (Bryan, Moran, Farrell & O'Brien, 2000) recommend that accurate, non-sensationalist information on the relative known risks associated with different types of drugs should be made available to all age groups. They also recommend that more positive attitudes towards those who misuse drugs should be promoted. This is important for the social integration of problem drug users and can influence their willingness to avail of treatment.

Not many qualitative research studies have been carried out on the general population of young people in Ireland. Such studies to date have tended to concentrate on problem drug use. It is important that there is a general awareness and, in particular, awareness among policy makers, of the social context of young people's drug taking, if suitable and appropriate prevention measures are to be adopted.

This chapter explores the research findings on drug use among the general population in Ireland.

3.2 Drug Consumption in the General Population

In 1998 a general population survey, Survey of Lifestyle, Attitudes and Nutrition (SLÁN) (Friel, Nic Gabhainn & Kelleher, 1999), was undertaken for the Department of Health and Children by the Centre for Health Promotion Studies, National University of Ireland (NUI), Galway. The results of the module on drug use are unpublished.[1]

---

1   Drug data from SLÁN were obtained through personal contact with the Centre for Health Promotion Studies, NUI, Galway.

This is the largest study undertaken in Ireland to date in which drug-use prevalence has been measured. The sampling frame used was the electoral register, the target population thus being adults aged 18 years and older. A proportionate random sampling design was used to select the survey sample. The questionnaires were posted to respondents and were self-administered. The sample size of the drug module of the survey was 10,415. The response rate was 62.2 per cent (n=6,539) (Friel, personal communication).

The findings indicate that cannabis was the most commonly-used drug, followed by amphetamines and ecstasy (see EMCDDA Standard Table 4.1 at Appendix 4, and Tables 3.1 and 3.2 below). The use of amphetamines was slightly higher than ecstasy use. Heroin was found to be the drug least used in the general population.

TABLE 3.1
Ireland 1998. SLÁN Survey. Last Twelve Months Prevalence.
Type of Drug by Age Groups. Percentages.

	Age Groups		
Type of Drug	18–64	18–34	18–24
Cannabis	9.4	17.7	26.0
Amphetamines	2.6	5.4	8.8
Ecstasy	2.4	4.9	8.1
LSD	1.4	2.9	5.1
Cocaine	1.3	2.6	3.4
Hypnotics and Sedatives*	1.2	1.4	2.1
Solvents	0.3	0.8	1.4
Heroin	0.3	0.7	0.8

Source: SLÁN, Centre for Health Promotion Studies, NUI, Galway.
* Includes benzodiazepines.

TABLE 3.2
Ireland 1998. SLÁN Survey. Lifetime, Last Twelve Months, and Last Thirty Days
Prevalence of Cannabis Use By Age Groups. Percentages.

	Age Groups		
Prevalence	18–64	18–34	18–24
Lifetime	19.9	30.0	33.4
Last 12 Months	9.4	17.7	26.0
Last 30 Days	5.1	9.7	15.3

Source: SLÁN, Centre for Health Promotion Studies, NUI, Galway.

The highest prevalence rate for cannabis use was found among 18- to 24-year-olds: 33.4 per cent had used cannabis at some time in the past; 26 per cent during the last twelve months; and 15.3 per cent in the last thirty days. The rates were lower in older age groups (see Table 3.2).

Young men under the age of 25 were the most likely to have used drugs. This was the case for all drug types in the 18- to 24-year-old age group (see EMCDDA Standard Table 4.1 at Appendix 4). In the older age groups, women were slightly more likely to have used hypnotics and sedatives, which include benzodiazepines. Interestingly, there were no gender differences in the 55- to 64-year-old age range for cannabis use during the past year and the past month, although the percentage was small at 0.5 per cent. Geographically, drug users were more likely to live in an urban location.

In the same year, 1998, a general population survey on drug-related knowledge, attitudes and beliefs (KAB1), using a much smaller sample (n=1,000), was undertaken by the DMRD (Bryan *et al.*, 2000). The fieldwork was carried out by an independent research organisation as part of a broader social omnibus survey. The aim of the survey was to investigate the attitudes of the general public towards drug use and drug users, and to determine the extent of cannabis use. As in the SLÁN study, the sampling frame used was the register of electors, the target population being adults aged 18 years and older. The sampling procedure was a two-stage, proportionate to size, random selection. The questionnaires were administered face-to-face in the respondents' homes. The response rate was 64.5 per cent. Prevalence information on lifetime use of cannabis only was collected. The findings of this survey (see EMCDDA Standard Table 4.2 at Appendix 4, and Table 3.3 below) were quite similar to those found in SLÁN, particularly in the case of the 18- to 24-year-old age group. As mentioned above, SLÁN found that lifetime prevalence of cannabis use among 18- to 24-year-olds was 33.4 per cent; the KAB1 figure was 32.3 per cent. Interestingly, no significant gender difference was found among the KAB1 18- to 24-year-olds: lifetime use of cannabis was 32.3 per cent for both males and females. The older age groups in the KAB1 survey showed somewhat lower prevalences than those found in SLÁN.

TABLE 3.3
Ireland 1998. KAB1 Survey. Lifetime Prevalence of Cannabis Use by Age Groups. Percentages.

Prevalence	Age Groups		
	18–64	18–34	18–24
Lifetime	14.2	26.2	32.3

Source: Bryan *et al.*, 2000.

3.3 School and Youth Population

There is more information available on drug use among school pupils, than among adults in the general population in Ireland. However, up to now most of the work has been carried out at regional level. The survey studies vary in a number of ways – objectives, methodologies, focus of data collection, questionnaire design, and age groups studied. As mentioned earlier, differences in theoretical approaches, reflecting different perspectives, can affect interpretations of survey results and can preclude meaningful comparisons. Therefore, the comparisons made below are tentative and must be viewed with these variations in mind.

In 1994 a survey of substance use among adolescents of school-going age (12- to 18-year-olds) was conducted in the Western Health Board (WHB) area (Kiernan, 1995). A sample of early school-leavers was also included in this study. Cannabis and solvents were the drugs most likely to have been used, with lifetime prevalence rates of 16 per cent and 14 per cent respectively (see Table 3.6).

In 1995, as part of the European Schools Survey Project on Alcohol and Other Drugs (ESPAD), nation-wide school surveys of 15- to 16-year-old (born in 1979) post-primary pupils were carried out in a number of European countries (Hibell et al., 1997: 12). In Ireland the data collection period was 10 March – 20 April 1995 (Hibell et al., 1997: 134). The Irish lifetime prevalence rate for cannabis use (ever having used) was found to be 37 per cent. This was among the highest found in all the countries participating in the study – the United Kingdom was higher at 40 per cent. However, this relatively high rate has not been found in subsequent surveys.

In 1996 a survey was carried out to examine lifestyles of second-level students in the Midland Health Board (MHB) area. The results were presented in a short report entitled 'Report on School Survey of Second-Level Students in the Midland Health Board Area' (Midland Health Board, 1996). A detailed description of the methodology was not provided. Twelve schools were randomly selected and 1,654 pupils completed a questionnaire in the classroom. Cannabis was the most widely-used drug, followed by solvents (see Table 3.6).

In 1998 a study of substance use among school pupils in the Dublin Metropolitan area was carried out as part of a European collaborative project called Drug Dependence: Risk and Monitoring (DDRAM). The stratified random sample consisted of 983 second-year students in sixteen schools (Brinkley, Fitzgerald & Greene, 1999). Last-month prevalence rates for cannabis and solvents were 15 per cent and 7 per cent respectively (see Table 3.7).

The latest national survey, the Health Behaviours in School-Aged Children (HBSC), was conducted in 1998 by the Centre for Health Promotion Studies, NUI, Galway; the drug module was unpublished (see EMCDDA Standard Table 4.3 at Appendix 4, and Tables 3.4 and 3.5 below).[2] The HBSC was a World Health Organisation collaborative study (Friel *et al.*, 1999). The sampling frame consisted of primary and post-primary schools, lists of which were provided by the Department of Education and Science. Pupils were selected using two-stage random sampling within health board areas and then in school classrooms. The sample size was 8,497; the response rate was 73 per cent. Respondents ranged in age from 9 to 17 years. Lifetime prevalence of cannabis use was found to be much less than the ESPAD finding of 37 per cent in 1995, at 21.7 per cent for 15- to 16-year-olds (see Table 3.4).

TABLE 3.4
Ireland 1998. Schools Survey – HBSC. Lifetime, Last Twelve Months, and Last Thirty Days Prevalence of Cannabis Use by Age Groups. Percentages.

	Age Groups			
Prevalence of Cannabis Use	11–12	13–14	15–16	17
Lifetime	3.0	8.0	21.7	28.5
Last 12 Months	2.3	6.5	18.3	24.0
Last 30 Days	1.3	4.3	10.5	11.0

Source: HBSC, Centre for Health Promotion Studies, NUI, Galway.

The highest prevalence was among 17-year-olds: 28.5 per cent had used cannabis at some time in the past (lifetime prevalence), 24 per cent had done so in the past twelve months and 11 per cent had used cannabis recently (in the past thirty days). All drug types were more likely to be used by males. However, in the case of lifetime use of cannabis, among 17-year-olds there was very little gender difference – male 28.7 per cent, female 28.5 per cent (see EMCDDA Standard Table 4.3 at Appendix 4). Details on experiences of using different types of drugs in the past twelve months (annual prevalence) were not collected.

Among young people in general (aged 9 to 17), after cannabis, solvents were the most commonly-used substances (see Table 3.5). Among 17-year-olds, prevalence of recent cannabis use (11%) was followed by amphetamine use (4.9%). Solvents (4.1%) were the

---

2   Drug data from HBSC were obtained through personal contact with the Centre for Health Promotion Studies, NUI, Galway.

next most commonly-used substances, and not ecstasy as might be expected. The recent prevalence of LSD use was similar to that of ecstasy use, at 3.7 per cent. The situation among younger age groups was shown to be quite different. Among 15- to 16-year-olds the use of cannabis (10.5%) and solvents (5.9%) was followed by amphetamine use (2.4%). Solvents were the substances most commonly used by 11- to 14-year-olds, followed by cannabis in the case of 13- to 14-year-olds. Surprisingly, among 11- to 12-year-olds, use of solvents (2.9%) was followed by cocaine use (1.9%), even before cannabis use (1.3%). Of particular concern was the recent cocaine use among 11- to 12-year-olds, which was the highest of all the age groups. Heroin use seems to have been higher than would be expected, especially among 17-year-olds at 2 per cent (see Table 3.5).

TABLE 3.5

**Ireland 1998. Schools Survey – HBSC. Last Thirty Days Prevalence.
Type of Drug by Age Groups. Percentages.**

| | Age Groups | | | | |
Type of Drug	11–12	13–14	15–16	17	9–17
Cannabis	1.3	4.3	10.5	11.0	5.9
Amphetamines	0.7	0.9	2.4	4.9	1.6
Ecstasy	0.6	0.9	1.9	3.7	1.3
LSD	0.8	0.9	1.7	3.7	1.3
Hypnotics & Sedatives*	0.8	1.4	1.9	2.1	1.4
Cocaine	1.9	1.6	1.5	1.8	1.7
Solvents	2.9	5.7	5.9	4.1	4.8
Heroin	0.8	0.8	1.0	2.0	0.9

Source: HBSC Survey, Centre for Health Promotion Studies, NUI, Galway.
* Includes tranquilisers or sedatives without prescription (barbs, jellies, downers).

In 1998 a school survey was conducted in the Eastern Health Board (EHB) area of the country (Rhatigan & Shelley, 1999). The purpose was to study the health behaviours of school pupils. Again, as for the HBSC, the sampling frame was the Department of Education and Science's lists of schools. A random sample of schools, stratified by county and school type, was selected. The sample size was 6,081 pupils aged between 10 and 18 years. The response rate was 78.2 per cent. Cannabis was the drug most commonly experienced at least once (lifetime), followed by solvents (see EMCDDA Standard Table 4.4 at Appendix 4, and Table 3.6 below). These data – lifetime use of cannabis (21%) and solvents (13%), and recent use of cannabis (11%) and solvents (7%) – are somewhat higher than the results from the HBSC survey. This might be expected, given that the sample was drawn from the most urbanised eastern region, including Dublin. Prevalence rates (both lifetime and recent) for cocaine use among the whole group are the same in both the HBSC and the EHB surveys, at 2 per cent.

Tables 3.6 and 3.7 below illustrate the difficulties involved in making comparisons between different studies. Attempting to compare youth surveys for different geographic locations, where different methodologies have been used, must be done with considerable caution. Drug use prevalence among young people also varies quite considerably according to the age groups examined. For example, in the HBSC survey the lifetime prevalence of cannabis use for the whole sample (9- to 17-year-olds) was 12 per cent (see Table 3.6), whereas for 15- to 16-year-olds it was 21.7 per cent (see Table 3.4), and for those aged 17 it was 28.5 per cent (see Table 3.4).

TABLE 3.6
Ireland 1995–1998. Comparison of School/Youth Surveys of Drug Use. Lifetime Prevalence of Drug Use by Type of Drug.

Survey/ Year	WHB 1994 (Local)	ESPAD 1995 (National)	MHB 1996 (Local)	HBSC 1998 (National)	EHB 1998 (Local)
Sample Size	2,762	1,849	1,654	8,497	6,081
Age Group	13–18	15–16	16–18	9–17	10–18
Drug Type					
Cannabis	16%	37%	26%	12%	21%
Amphetamines	2%	3%	5%	3%	5%
Ecstasy	2%	9%	7%	2%	3%
LSD or Other Hallucinogens	9%	13%	9%	4%	3%
Hypnotics & Sedatives	2%	7%	4%	3%	3%
Cocaine	1%	2%*	NA	2%	2%
Solvents	14%	19%	17%	10%	13%
Heroin	1%	2%	NA	1%	1%

* 3% also claimed to have ever used crack.
NA = No data available.

The results from the 1995 ESPAD survey show higher prevalence rates for most drug types. In fact, the results of this survey give the highest prevalence rates of all school surveys conducted in Ireland to date. No explanation for this is immediately evident, but it may be partly due to methodological differences in the research, or it could possibly reflect a fall in drug use by young people. However, the fact that, in this survey conducted in 1995, 5 per cent claimed to have used cocaine and crack (cocaine 2% and crack 3%), and the relatively high recent prevalence rates for cocaine use found in the HBSC survey, indicate that further study of cocaine use among young people is required.

TABLE 3.7

Ireland 1995–1998. Comparison of School/Youth Surveys of Drug Use. Last Thirty Days Prevalence of Drug Use by Type of Drug.

Survey/ Year	WHB 1994 (Local)	ESPAD 1995 (National)	MHB 1996 (Local)	HBSC 1998 (National)	EHB 1998 (Local)	DDRAM 1998 (Local)
Sample Size	2,762	1,849	1,654	8,497	6,081	983
Age Group	13–18	15–16	16–18	9–17	10–18	14–15
Drug Type						
Cannabis	9%	19%	NA	6%	11%	15%
Amphetamines	1%	NA	NA	2%	3%	NA
Ecstasy	1%	NA	NA	1%	3%	NA
LSD	NA	NA	NA	1%	2%	NA
Hypnotics & Sedatives	NA	NA	NA	2%	2%	NA
Cocaine	1%	NA	NA	2%	2%	NA
Solvents	NA	NA	NA	5%	7%	7%
Heroin	0%	NA	NA	1%	1%	NA

NA = No data available.

In conclusion, it emerges that drug use is more prevalent among young Dublin males. What also transpires is the importance of carrying out prevalence surveys using comparable methodologies, if meaningful comparisons are to be made. Also, information on recent use (past thirty days/past month) of drugs is not always as readily available as lifetime use (ever used), even though it is usually a better indication of the current situation.

3.4 Drug Consumption in Specific Groups

Research has found that a significant proportion of Ireland's prison population has a history of drug use, and that a number of prisoners continue to use drugs while incarcerated. Two recent studies (Allwright, Barry, Bradley, Long & Thornton, 1999; Long *et al.*, 2000), concerned with the prevalence of HIV, hepatitis B and hepatitis C among the Irish prison population, explored the related risk behaviours and drug use engaged in by prisoners. Allwright *et al.* (1999) found that of 1,205 respondents, 630 (52.3%) reported that they had used heroin. The authors concluded 'drug use within prison was common' (Allwright *et al.*, 1999: 18). The subsequent study of a sample (n=604) of committal[3] prisoners found lower rates of prisoners reporting drug use (Long *et al.*, 2000). Of the sample, 35.5 per cent reported that they had ever smoked heroin and/or injected drugs. Both of these studies suggest that there is a significant proportion of prisoners who have a history of drug use and, furthermore, a significant proportion continues to engage in illicit drug use once incarcerated.

While nothing is known about either the extent to which illicit drug use occurs within minority groupings in Ireland, or the nature of this use, anecdotal evidence suggests that there is a need to explore drug use in this context. It is important that the necessary information be available to facilitate Irish services to address any specific needs that drug users from minority groups may have, and to offer services in a way that will encourage these users to access them.

3.5 Prevalence of Problem Drug Use in the General Population

Studies of national and local prevalence estimates of problem drug use are quite limited in Ireland. An exploratory study was carried out (Comiskey, 1998) to estimate the prevalence of problematic opiate use in Dublin. Using the capture/re-capture methodology, with *three* samples of data (methadone treatment list, hospital inpatient data, and Garda record data), this local study estimated that there were between 12,037 and 14,804 opiate users in Dublin in 1996. There were difficulties with the samples used in this study – 22 per cent of the Garda sample contained ambiguous data (7% were non-opiate users; 10% were included because they were found to be in possession of an opiate; and 5% were identified by unspecified means). The Garda data were originally collected for a study to examine drug-related crime (Keogh, 1997), with different definitions to those used in the prevalence study. Prevalence studies such as this should be regarded as an exploratory exercise in the development of methodologies to estimate

---

3   Committal prisoners were defined as 'prisoners who have been admitted to the prison within the preceding 48 hours, accused or guilty of a new crime, excluding those on temporary release or transferred from another prison. The committal population includes individuals entering on remand, following sentence, committed as a result of a bench warrant, and non-nationals without valid documentation.' (Long *et al.*, 2000: 2).

the prevalence of problem drug use, and the resultant estimates should be viewed in this light (see Chapter 5).

Another local-area prevalence study was carried out in north-east inner city Dublin, an area with higher than average levels of social and economic disadvantage. This study (Coveney, Murphy-Lawless, Redmond & Sheridan, 1999) collected data from four sources: five treatment and support agencies; agency waiting lists; a residents' street survey; and two general practitioners. Of the 1,657 individuals identified, 477 were residents of the Dublin 1 postal district (north inner city). It was estimated that the prevalence rate of heroin use was 2 per cent of the population of that area. This is surprisingly low, given that it is considered to be a high-risk area, but is probably a reflection of the methodology used in the study.

3.6 Summary

The lifetime experience of drug use (respondents reporting that they have used at some time in the past) in the general population of young people in Ireland is widespread, but this does not necessarily mean that drug use among such young people is lasting.

What is evident from surveys conducted in recent years (SLÁN; HBSC; Rhatigan & Shelley, 1999; Hibell *et al.*, 1997; Kiernan, 1995) is that alcohol and tobacco are the most widely-used drugs in Irish society. Cannabis is the most commonly-used illicit drug, followed by amphetamines and ecstasy, and their use is widespread. Whether drug use is increasing, is not clear from general population survey data. Even among young people of school-going age, it is difficult to identify trends from survey results of the past two years. The much-quoted, relatively high lifetime prevalence of cannabis use (37%) among 15- to 16-year-old school pupils (Hibell *et al.*, 1997) has not been sustained in more recent school surveys (HBSC; Rhatigan & Shelley, 1999). This could reflect a fall in drug use by young people.

From the available research it is apparent that, generally speaking, young men in urban areas are the most likely to have misused drugs, mainly cannabis. However, a distinction must be made between the adult population and young people. Among adults over 18 years of age, after cannabis, amphetamines and ecstasy are the drugs most commonly used, although to a much lesser extent. On the other hand, among young people up to 18, there is some disparity between different age groups. For example, among young people in general (aged 9 to 18), after cannabis, solvents are the most widely-used substances. However, adolescents between 11 and 14 years of age are more likely to use solvents. The relatively high prevalence rates for cocaine use among young people up to 16 years of age requires further exploration. Heroin, which is generally considered to be the drug that causes the most problems for individuals, communities and society, is the drug least used in the general population.

Research findings indicate that a significant proportion of Ireland's prison population has a history of drug use, and that a number of prisoners continue to use drugs while incarcerated.

Nothing is known about either the extent to which illicit drug use occurs within minority groups or the nature of this use. There is a need to carry out research into drug use in this context, in order to facilitate the provision of accessible drug treatment services.

The objectives and methodologies used in general population surveys to study the extent of drug use in Ireland vary. Therefore, comparisons are tentative and must be viewed with these variations in mind. If meaningful interpretations and comparisons are to be made, a priority for future work should be to carry out prevalence surveys in general populations using comparable methodologies. Information on recent and annual use should be available, as well as lifetime experience of drug use. Where possible, surveys should be comparable nationally as well as in the wider European context. It is also important that these surveys be replicated at frequent intervals, if trends over time are to be monitored.

Methodologies to estimate the prevalence of problem drug use are at an exploratory stage and the findings emerging from studies using such methodologies should be viewed as very crude estimates.

3.7 References

Allwright, S., Barry, J., Bradley, F., Long, J. & Thornton, L. (1999). *Hepatitis B, Hepatitis C and HIV in Irish Prisoners: Prevalence and risk*. Dublin: The Stationery Office.

Brinkley, A., Fitzgerald, M. & Greene, S. (1999). 'Substance Use in Early Adolescence: A Study of the Rates and Patterns of Substance Use among Pupils in Dublin'. Unpublished. Project supported by Eastern Health Board and co-financed by the European Commission.

Bryan, A., Moran, R., Farrell, E. & O'Brien, M. (2000). *Drug-Related Knowledge, Attitudes and Beliefs in Ireland. Report of a nation-wide survey*. Dublin: The Health Research Board.

Comiskey, C. (1998). 'Estimating the Prevalence of Opiate Use in Dublin, Ireland, during 1996'. Unpublished document.

Coveney, E., Murphy-Lawless, J., Redmond. D. & Sheridan, S. (1999). *Prevalence, Profiles and Policy. A case study of drug use in north inner city Dublin*. Dublin: North Inner City Drug Task Force.

Friel, S., Nic Gabhainn, S. & Kelleher, C. (1999). *The National Health & Lifestyle Surveys*. Dublin and Galway: Health Promotion Unit, Department of Health and Children, Dublin, and Centre for Health Promotion Studies, NUI, Galway.

Hibell, B., Andersson, B., Bjarnason, T., Kokkevi, A., Morgan, M. & Narusk, A. (1997). *The 1995 ESPAD Report. Alcohol and other drug use among students in 26 European countries*. Stockholm and Strasbourg: The Swedish Council for Alcohol and other Drugs (CAN), Stockholm, and Council of Europe, Pompidou Group, Strasbourg.

Keogh, E. (1997). *Illicit Drug Use & Related Criminal Activity in the Dublin Metropolitan Area*. Dublin: An Garda Síochána.

Kiernan, R. (1995). *Report on Substance Use among Adolescents in the Western Health Board*. Galway: Western Health Board.

Long, J., Allwright, S., Barry, J., Reaper-Reynolds, S., Thornton, L. & Bradley, F. (2000). *Hepatitis B, Hepatitis C and HIV in Irish Prisoners, Part II: Prevalence and risk in committal prisoners 1999*. Dublin: The Stationery Office.

Midland Health Board (1996). 'Report on School Survey of Second-Level Students in the Midland Health Board Area'. Unpublished document.

Nic Gabhainn, S. & Walsh, F. (2000). Drug prevention: Perspectives on family and community interventions. In P. Dolan, J. Canavan & J. Pinkerton (eds) *Family Support: Direction from diversity*. London: Jessica Kingsley.

Rhatigan, A. & Shelley, E. (1999). *Health Behaviours of School Pupils in the Eastern Health Board*. Dublin: Eastern Health Board.

CHAPTER 4

HEALTH ISSUES AND CONSEQUENCES OF DRUG MISUSE

MARY O'BRIEN AND LUCY DILLON

4.1 Introduction

Drug misuse can have a number of serious consequences for the health of the individual drug user. Infectious diseases such as HIV and hepatitis C can reach a high prevalence among injecting drug users (IDUs). Drug-related mortality is another possible consequence of some forms of drug use.

People encountering very serious problems with drug misuse will more than likely eventually come into contact with drug treatment services. The treated population of drug users in Ireland is well represented in the National Drug Treatment Reporting System (NDTRS). This is an epidemiological database providing anonymous data on people who receive treatment for problem drug use. The data are collected from both statutory and voluntary drug treatment agencies throughout the country by the Drug Misuse Research Division (DMRD) of the Health Research Board (HRB).

In recent years there has been an expansion in the services provided for problem drug users. Compared to ten years ago services are now decentralised and have become more diversified and dispersed both locally and nationally. Problematic opiate use, mainly heroin, continues to be concentrated in the Dublin area, in localities with high levels of social and economic disadvantage. Pockets of heroin use are being reported in recent times in a number of areas throughout the country. Analysis of the characteristics of clients presenting to treatment for the first time gives a good indication of trends over a number of years.

This chapter explores health issues and consequences of drug misuse under the following headings:

4.2 Characteristics of Clients, Patterns of Use and Trends
4.3 Drug-Related Risk Behaviours and Trends
4.4 Drug-Related Infectious Diseases
4.5 Other Drug-Related Morbidity
4.6 Drug-Related Mortality

4.2 Characteristics of Clients, Patterns of Use and Trends

Drug-use patterns in Ireland vary according to geographic location. Problem opiate use, mostly heroin, is mainly confined to the Dublin area. This is beginning to change, with pockets of heroin use now becoming apparent in a number of urbanised areas in regional locations. While the profile of the typical problematic drug user – young, unemployed male, leaving school at an early age and living in a socially and economically disadvantaged area – has not varied much over the years, there has been a change in some trends over the past five years.

Data on clients presenting for treatment for the first time are presented in Table 4.1 for the five-year period 1995–1999. Gender distribution has not changed much over the five-year period, and the mean age has remained fairly stable at around 22 years. Over 70 per cent of those presenting for treatment for the first time are under 25 years old. This is younger than in other EU countries and is a reflection of the demographic situation in Ireland, where the median age of the Irish population is much younger than the EU average. Nearly half the population in Ireland (48%) is under 30 years of age (see Table 2.1 at Appendix 2), whereas the median age in other EU countries is between 35 and 40 years of age.

Between 1995 and 1999 there was a fall in the proportion of clients living in the parental home (see Table 4.1). There was a decrease in those who left school before the age of 16 years, from 51.8 per cent in 1995 to 43.2 per cent in 1999. There was a sizeable increase in the level of employment among problem drug users, from a very low 15.2 per cent in 1995 to 31.2 per cent in 1999, reflecting more general changes in Irish society in relation to improvements in the economy, *inter alia*, over the same period. The mean age of initial drug use was between 15 and16 years of age and did not change much over the five-year period. Heroin was the main drug of misuse for over half of those presenting for treatment for the first time. Over the five-year period there was an increase in the proportion injecting their main drug of misuse, which was mainly heroin.

TABLE 4.1

Ireland 1995–1999. New Clients Presenting for Treatment. Characteristics and Patterns of Use.

Characteristics	1995	1996	1997	1998	1999
Valid N	1,870	2,014	1,465	1,621	1,636
Gender Ratio (Male:Female)	80:20	73:27	72:28	74:26	73:27
Mean Age	21.1	21.3	22.0	22.1	22.7
Living Status – with Parental Family	79.0%	76.5%	71.6%	71.1%	70.2%
Early School-Leavers (<16 Years Old)	51.8%	50.2%	45.8%	45.2%	43.2%
Regular Employment	15.2%	13.9%	19.5%	24.8%	31.2%
Mean Age First Used any Drug (excl. Alcohol)	15.6	15.4	16.0	15.5	15.7
Main Drug – Heroin	54.6%	63.2%	58.4%	55.7%	53.5%
Main Drug – Route of Administration – Inject	23.8%	24.3%	29.3%	28.8%	30.6%

Source: NDTRS, DMRD, HRB.

The most recent data available indicate that there is great disparity in the pattern of drug use in different parts of the country. Problematic opiate/heroin use occurs mainly in the eastern region of the country, around Dublin. Seven out of ten Irish clients receiving drug treatment are residents of the Eastern Health Board (EHB) area (now three health boards in the Eastern Regional Health Authority (ERHA)) (O'Brien, Moran, Kelleher & Cahill, 2000). Most of these clients (80%) are treated for heroin misuse (O'Brien *et al.*, 2000). In other health board areas throughout the country cannabis is the drug for which the majority of people receive treatment (O'Brien *et al.*, 2000). The characteristics of clients vary according to the types of drugs being used. Heroin users are much less likely to be still at school than cannabis users; and they are more likely to be involved in behaviours with detrimental effects on their health, such as injecting and sharing injecting equipment.

Trends in problem drug use vary according to the type of drug involved. Information on treatment demand for different drugs presented below was obtained from the NDTRS.

Heroin – A majority of people (around six out of ten new cases each year) presenting to drug treatment services have problems with the misuse of heroin, that is, heroin is the main drug of misuse. This is mainly confined to the Dublin area. A sizeable proportion (56% in 1999) of those presenting to treatment services for the first time with problem heroin use are involved in intravenous drug-using practices, with very serious health and social consequences. This is the highest level in the past five years (38% in 1995; 37% in 1996; 49% in 1997; 50% in 1998) (see EMCDDA Standard Table 4.6 at Appendix 4).

Cannabis – Since the NDTRS was set up in 1990, the percentage of people presenting for treatment for cannabis use has not varied much: between 11 and 16 per cent. After heroin, cannabis is the drug, at a much lower level, for which treatment is most commonly sought. More than half of cannabis misusers (55%) started to use cannabis between the ages of 15 and 19; 37 per cent started before the age of 15 (Moran, O'Brien & Duff, 1997).

Cocaine – Treatment demand for problem cocaine use has always been relatively low – between 1 and 2 per cent. Apart from addiction counselling, there are no specific treatments for problem cocaine users in Ireland. Of all those presenting for treatment for the first time in 1999 with multiple drug problems (more than one drug) (64%), 7 per cent were seeking treatment for problem cocaine use.

Synthetic Drugs – Demand for treatment for problem ecstasy use has decreased somewhat in recent years, from 11 per cent in 1995 to 8.8 per cent in 1999. The proportion of problem amphetamine users presenting for treatment for the first time has increased from 0.4 per cent in 1995 to 2.1 per cent in 1999. A worrying development is that in 1999, 6 per cent of these were injecting the drug. The proportion presenting with problem LSD use has been falling over the past five years, from 1.6 per cent in 1995 to 0.2 per cent in 1999.

The majority of people presenting for treatment for drug use problems in Ireland are treated at non-residential drug treatment centres. Data from the NDTRS for 1999 show the following percentages presenting to different types of treatment services: 57 per cent to non-residential; 34 per cent to residential; 6 per cent to low-threshold services; 3 per cent to medical doctors in general practice. It should be stressed that in 1999 only a minority of general practitioners (GPs) in private practice were reporting to the NDTRS, and contacts in prisons were very poorly represented. Men are more likely to be receiving treatment at residential or low-threshold services, while women are more likely to present to non-residential or GP services for treatment. Clients living in the parental home are least likely to be attending low-threshold services. Unemployed clients are the most likely to be attending low-threshold services; those in regular employment are more likely to be receiving treatment from a GP.

Against a background of increasing encouragement for GPs to become more involved in the treatment of drug users, a study was carried out in a specialised drug treatment setting, during August–September 1997, to assess the utilisation of primary care services for general health purposes by injecting opiate users (n=77) (Smyth, McMahon, O'Connor & Ryan, 1999b). A structured questionnaire was used to interview clients. The sample size was 139, with a response rate of 75 per cent. The sampling procedure was opportunistic. Despite general policy changes, such as more emphasis on harm minimisation, the findings were similar to those of an equivalent study in 1991. In particular, the relative frequency of GP and hospital accident and emergency (A&E) department attendances was unchanged. Concern was expressed by the authors (Smyth *et al.*, 1999b) at the high proportion being prescribed benzodiazepines (39%) by GPs. They stated that this indicated that there was 'clearly a wide gap' between treatment approaches by psychiatrists, specialising in substance misuse at treatment centres, and GPs, in the management of co-morbid disorders such as anxiety and sleep disorders among drug users. The need for improved communication and co-operation, as well as explicit protocols relating to clarity, consistency and continuity in treatment approaches, was stressed.

In 2000 the Minister for Health and Children set up a committee to examine benzodiazepine-prescribing trends in Ireland. This committee will examine current prescribing trends and will make recommendations on good prescribing practice, particularly in relation to drug misusers.

4.3   Drug-Related Risk Behaviours and Trends

Risk behaviours are very important in the transmission of drug-related infectious diseases (HIV, hepatitis B, hepatitis C). Injecting with shared equipment is the crucial transmission route among IDUs; sexual contact is likely to be the most common transmission route among the wider population. A retrospective examination of data from the Needle Exchange Programme (NEP) in the EHB area was carried out to identify the factors associated with high-risk behaviours (Mullen & Barry, 1999).

The NEP was set up in 1989. Drug users who attended for the first time between 1990 and 1997 were included (N=6,025). The number of first attenders increased from 350 in 1990 to 1,039 in 1997. Four needles, on average, were distributed to first attenders; all were offered condoms, and 45 per cent accepted. First-time attenders were predominantly male, but over the eight-year period the proportion of women increased from 18 per cent in 1990 to 24 per cent in 1997; the increase in the number of women was particularly noticeable in young women under 20 years of age. The mean number of years of injecting drug use among the study group was four years. The overall prevalence of needle sharing in the year prior to attendance was 39 per cent, but women (44%) were more likely to share than men (38%). Women (51%) were also more likely to engage in unsafe sex than men (44%). Young injectors, under 20 years of age, were just as likely as all attenders to share injecting equipment (39%). Those who did not share injecting equipment were more likely to use condoms, than those who did share. Young attenders, under 20 years of age, were less likely to be involved in unsafe sex than the overall group (see Table 4.2).

TABLE 4.2
Eastern Health Board Area 1990–1997.
Characteristics and Risk Behaviours of Needle Exchange Attenders.

Characteristics and Risk Behaviours Years	All Attenders	Young Attenders < 20
Total (N)	6,025	1,224
Gender Ratio:		
Overall Male:Female	80:20	75:25
1990 Male:Female	82:18	86:14
1997 Male:Female	76:24	68:32
Mean Age	25	18.6
Risk Behaviours:		
Injecting – Mean Number of Years	4	<1
Sharing Prevalence – Past Year::		
Total	39%	39%
Male	38%	NA
Female	44%	NA
Unsafe Sex:		
Male	44%	36%
Female	51%	48%

Source: Mullen *et al.*, 1999.
NA = Data not available.

Trends over the time period 1990 – 1997 showed a significant decrease in high-risk behaviours: needle-sharing practices fell and safe sex (use of condoms) practices increased. Women engaged in more risky behaviours, and, with the proportion of women in the drug-using population increasing over time, this has serious health implications. Young IDUs are a particularly at-risk group. However, they do seem to present quite early in their drug-using careers to needle exchange programmes. The authors stated that 'it is crucial that young people do not encounter barriers to protecting themselves, such as parental permission, mandatory treatment, and statutory notification' (Mullen *et al.*, 1999: 29). The authors argued that this would defeat the purpose of a low-threshold service, to which young people are more likely to present. The profile of the attenders at the NEP highlights the importance of providing prevention and early intervention programmes, particularly for young people. The authors recommended that more in-depth and qualitative research was needed to increase understanding of IDUs – 'the issues surrounding drug use, risk management and sexual relationships' (Mullen *et al.*, 1999: 25) – in order to make prevention strategies more effective.

Another study also highlights the fact that women are a very at-risk group among drug users (Geoghegan, O'Shea & Cox, 1999). Taking a somewhat different perspective and focusing on gender differences, the research study, carried out at the Merchant's Quay Project in Dublin (a voluntary agency providing a number of services to drug users, including a needle exchange service), explored patterns of drug use, risk behaviour, health and well-being among 934 new attenders. Data were collected between May 1997 and April 1998, from all new clients. A sizeable minority was female (25%) and notable gender differences were found. Women were younger than men and were more likely to:

- have a sexual partner who was an IDU;
- be living with an IDU;
- share injecting equipment with their sexual partner;
- report recent sharing of injecting paraphernalia;
- report having problems finding an intravenous site;
- report having abscesses and to be suffering from weight loss;
- report depression, being unable to cope, feeling isolated and having suicidal tendencies;
- have attended a GP in the previous three months; and
- have a medical card.

Heroin was the preferred drug of choice of all the study participants; a majority (86%) of the overall group reported that they had smoked heroin prior to injecting; no gender difference was found. However, women had significantly shorter smoking careers and were more likely to present sooner in their injecting careers to treatment services than men. The authors concluded that this research illustrated that it is important to recognise that women drug users do exist and that they 'are more likely than their male counterparts to engage in risk behaviour which has a detrimental effect on their mental and physical health' (Geoghegan *et al.*, 1999: 135).

Data from the NDTRS were used in a study (Smyth, O'Brien & Barry, 2000) to examine trends in treated opiate use and to identify factors associated with the route of administration of heroin. Dublin clients presenting for the first time for treatment of an opiate problem over the six-year period 1991 – 96 were included. The study population was 3,981. Over the period there was a three-fold increase in the number of new clients and the proportion of females increased. The mean age of first opiate use declined and users began presenting for treatment earlier in their opiate-using careers. There was an increase in the proportion of heroin users as distinct from users of other opiates, such as morphine sulphate tablets. There was a dramatic increase in heroin smoking between 1994 and 1996, when it became the most common route of administering heroin. Heroin was most likely to be smoked by young employed people who were using heroin for less than three years.

The reasons for the increase in chasing (heroin smoking) between 1994 and 1996 are not clear. It was suggested that, while awareness of AIDS and the risks of injecting might have been factors, it would be simplistic to assume that this, alone, accounted for the change in the pattern of heroin use (Smyth *et al.*, 2000). In a later study of first-time attenders at a needle exchange programme between May 1997 and February 1998, a comparative analysis of the risk behaviour of younger and older injectors, i.e. under 25 and over 25 years of age, was carried out. It was found that the younger group (under 25 years old) was significantly more likely to have smoked illicit drugs prior to injecting and to report using heroin as their primary drug (Cassin, Geoghegan & Cox, 1998). It might be that smoking was the preferred route for young people starting to use heroin, particularly for those reluctant to use injecting equipment. The more acceptable nature of chasing, it was suggested, might attract increasing numbers to use heroin, and concern was expressed that 'chasing may prove to be a dragon in sheep's clothing' (Smyth *et al.*, 2000: 1223).

Data from the NDTRS for 1997 – 1999 suggest that these concerns were warranted. The data (see EMCDDA Standard Table 4.5 at Appendix 4) show that between 1990 and 1996 the percentage of 'all contacts' injecting heroin decreased from 88 per cent to 49 per cent. However, since then the percentage has been increasing, from 64 per cent in 1997 to 69 per cent in 1999. The increasing injecting trend is also true for those receiving treatment for the first time (see EMCDDA Standard Table 4.6 at Appendix 4). Between 1990 and 1996 the percentage of 'first contact' drug users injecting heroin decreased from 83 per cent to 37 per cent, but it increased from 49 per cent in 1997, to 50 per cent in 1998 and 56 per cent in 1999. The explanation is likely to be a complex one, involving many factors (for example, sub-group norms/perceptions, availability, price of drugs), but it may be that young people, who initially are reluctant to inject and prefer to smoke, are more willing to inject once heroin use has become habitual.

In a qualitative study of prisoners (n=29) it was found that moving from smoking to injecting heroin was motivated by the need for a more efficient use of a scarce commodity. Because of the limited quantity of heroin available in prison, drug-using prisoners managed their drug use in order to ensure that the maximum number of people was facilitated by the heroin that could be accessed. Since smoking was considered to be wasteful, injecting rather than smoking heroin was more acceptable. Furthermore, injecting was perceived to give a better 'buzz' than smoking, once an individual had become a habitual user (Dillon, forthcoming).

A further trend of note was found in a study of seventy-seven drug-using women (O'Neill & O'Connor, 1999) involved in prostitution. The women in the study were found to be a particularly vulnerable and marginalised group, who engaged in high-risk behaviours. The following were the findings:

- 45 per cent started working in prostitution between the ages of 13 and 19 years, mainly to earn money for drugs;
- 83 per cent had injected in the past month, and a quarter of these (n=16) had shared needles in the past month; and
- less than one-third had been screened for sexually-transmitted diseases.

Compared to similar research carried out in 1996 (in O'Neill et al., 1999: 9) the women in the 1999 study:

- tended to be younger;
- were more likely to have their children being cared for by someone else; and
- were more likely to be homeless.

These findings point to the importance of more imaginative education initiatives in harm-reduction interventions. This was demonstrated by a study conducted in a specialised treatment setting (Smyth, McMahon, O'Connor & Ryan, 1999a). The level of knowledge of IDUs regarding hepatitis C and the factors influencing this knowledge were assessed, using an instrument developed by the research team. The results showed that there were prominent misconceptions about the cause of transmission and natural history of hepatitis C infection. Contact with services did not lead to any significant gain in understanding. The authors concluded that current education approaches used in specialist treatment centres and by GPs were deficient. They recommended a move away from the 'typical didactic model of fact provision' (Smyth et al., 1999a: 263) to a more explorative approach, where misconceptions were more likely to emerge, thereby providing the opportunity to correct and educate.

4.4 Drug-Related Infectious Diseases[1]

Drug-related infectious diseases present issues of concern for public health. HIV/AIDS and hepatitis B and C are the main diseases of concern. While anecdotal evidence suggests that tuberculosis may be increasing among Irish drug users, no routine data is available and the focus of research and public health concerns remains in the areas of HIV and hepatitis. This section explores the data relating to each of the following drug-related infectious diseases – HIV and AIDS, hepatitis B and hepatitis C.

HIV and AIDS

The majority of data collected on drug-related infectious diseases relate to HIV. Two main sources of data are discussed below: first, the routine data on HIV tests reported by the Department of Health and Children; and second, special studies that have estimated the prevalence of HIV among drug users, mainly in treatment settings.

In Ireland, the Department of Health and Children, in collaboration with the Virus Reference Laboratory, located in University College, Dublin (UCD), produces statistics on HIV tests, which are issued every six months. The figures relating to HIV tests are broken down according to risk category. There are a number of risk categories identified in relation to HIV infection, including injecting drug use, homosexual sex and haemophiliac contact. Therefore, it is possible to get a breakdown of the number of HIV-positive cases attributable to injecting drug use in a given year.

The cumulative figures for the HIV-positive cases, from the start of data collection in 1982 up until 1985, show that just over 60 per cent (n=221) of all positive cases (N=363) were attributed to injecting drug use (see Table 4.3). Since 1985, injecting drug use has continued to be one of the main risk categories, accounting for 41.6 per cent of the cumulative number of positive cases up until 31 December 1999 (see Table 4.3).

The proportion of positive cases attributed to the 'intravenous drug user' (IVDU) category generally decreased from 1992 through to 1998. In 1994, for the first time, intravenous drug use accounted for fewer new positive cases than the 'homosexual sex' or 'heterosexual sex and/or risk unspecified' categories (see Table 4.3). In fact, the proportion of positive HIV tests attributed to intravenous drug use fell from 49.1 per cent in 1989, to a low of 17.7 per cent in 1997 (see Table 4.3). It is suggested that the

---

1   The following is a summary of a paper on drug-related infectious diseases in Ireland, which will appear in a forthcoming publication from the Drug Misuse Research Division (DMRD) of the Health Research Board (HRB).

reduction, both proportionately and in absolute numbers, over this period may be attributed, at least in part, to the expansion of services aimed at reducing the spread of HIV among IDUs, i.e. substitution and needle exchange programmes.

Despite the apparent reduction in the proportion of positive cases attributed to injecting drug use and the actual number of positive tests, figures from 1999 show a substantial increase in the number of positive cases. Between 1998 and 1999 the total number of new cases of HIV increased from 136 to 209. Furthermore, the number of new positive cases attributed to injecting drug use increased from twenty-six of the total new cases (N=136) in 1998 to sixty-nine of the new cases (N=209) in 1999. Therefore, proportionately, injecting drug use as a risk category increased from accounting for 19.1 per cent of new HIV-positive cases within this data source in 1998, to 33 per cent in 1999. This is the highest annual proportion of new positive cases attributed to injecting drug use since 1993.

TABLE 4.3
Ireland 1985–1999. HIV-Positive Cases by Risk Category.
Numbers and Percentages.

Year	IVDUs		Homosexual Sex		Heterosexual Sex /Risk Unspecified		Other		Total	
	n	(%)	n	(%)	n	(%)	n	(%)	n	(%)
1985[*]	221	(60.9)	39	(10.7)	0		103	(28.4)	363	(100.0)
1986	112	(66.3)	11	(6.5)	21	(12.5)	25	(14.8)	169	(100.0)
1987	72	(49.7)	21	(14.5)	26	(17.9)	26	(17.9)	145	(100.0)
1988	58	(50.4)	17	(14.8)	20	(17.4)	20	(17.4)	115	(100.0)
1989	57	(49.1)	33	(28.5)	0		26	(22.4)	116	(100.0)
1990	50	(45.1)	25	(22.5)	24	(21.6)	12	(10.8)	111	(100.0)
1991	34	(36.9)	27	(29.4)	25	(27.2)	6	(6.5)	92	(100.0)
1992	82	(40.8)	58	(28.9)	50	(24.9)	11	(5.5)	201	(100.1)
1993	52	(38.0)	48	(35.0)	21	(15.3)	16	(11.7)	137	(100.0)
1994	20	(23.5)	31	(36.5)	22	(25.9)	12	(14.1)	85	(100.0)
1995	19	(20.9)	33	(36.3)	30	(33.0)	9	(9.9)	91	(100.1)
1996	20	(18.9)	41	(38.7)	27	(25.5)	18	(17.0)	106	(100.1)
1997	21	(17.7)	37	(31.1)	40	(33.6)	21	(17.7)	119	(100.1)
1998	26	(19.1)	37	(27.2)	47	(34.6)	26	(19.1)	136	(100.0)
1999	69	(33.0)	40	(19.1)	59	(28.2)	41	(19.6)	209	(99.9)
Total	**913**	**(41.6)**	**498**	**(22.7)**	**412**	**(18.8)**	**372**	**(17.0)**	**2,195**	**(100.1)**

Source: Routine HIV/AIDS statistics compiled by the Virus Research Laboratory and reported to the Department of Health and Children.
* Cumulative figures for 1982 – 1985.

Gender is the only socio-demographic data collected on those who are tested for HIV from the Department of Health and Children's data source; gender has been reported since 1997. An examination of the figures by gender suggests a possible change in the gender distribution of those who are testing positive for HIV in Ireland (see Table 4.4). In 1997 females only accounted for three of the twenty-one new positive cases attributed to injecting drug use. In 1998 this had increased to ten of the twenty-six positive cases among IDUs, and in 1999 it had increased further to account for thirty-four of the sixty-nine positive cases. Speaking in percentage terms, women have increased from representing 14.3 per cent of the positive tests among IDUs in 1997, to 38.5 per cent in 1998 and 49.3 per cent in 1999. Owing to the lack of information on gender prior to 1997, it is not possible to explore trends over a more extended period of time. Anecdotal evidence suggests that these figures may reflect a real increase in the number of women IDUs who are becoming infected with HIV. However, it is also suggested that these women may be becoming infected through their sexual behaviour rather than through their injecting drug use. Once identified as an IDU, however, their infection will tend to be attributed to their injecting drug-using behaviour. Anecdotal evidence also suggests that a growing number of women may be presenting for testing in order to be able to minimise the risk of infection to their baby were they to become pregnant.

TABLE 4.4

Ireland 1997–1999. HIV Seropositive IDUs by Gender. Numbers and Percentages.

Year	Male		Female		Total	
	n	(%)	n	(%)	n	(%)
1997	18	(85.7)	3	(14.3)	21	(100)
1998	16	(61.5)	10	(38.5)	26	(100)
1999	35	(50.7)	34	(49.3)	69	(100)

Source: Routine HIV/AIDS statistics compiled by the Virus Research Laboratory and reported to the Department of Health and Children.

Since recording began in 1982 and up until 31 December 1999, there have been 691 AIDS cases reported in Ireland, and 349 AIDS-related deaths (see Table 3.2 at Appendix 3). In 1999 there were forty-one new AIDS-related cases recorded. IDUs continue to represent one of the main risk categories recorded in this data source. In 1999, IDUs accounted for 39 per cent of new AIDS cases, and 41 per cent of the year's AIDS-related deaths.

A number of special studies have been carried out exploring the prevalence of HIV among drug users in a range of study locations, mainly in treatment settings. The studies include drug users located in the community, in drug treatment centres, in needle exchange programmes and in prisons. Prevalence rates range from 65 per cent among a cohort of IDUs who were first identified in 1985 and who were monitored over the next decade (O'Kelly & Bury, 1996), to 3.5 per cent among a national cohort of prisoners (Allwright *et al.*, 1999). A summary of the research findings on the prevalence of HIV infection among drug users is presented in Table 4.5 below.

TABLE 4.5

Ireland 1991–1999. Summary of Research Findings on the Prevalence of HIV Infection among Particular Cohorts of Drug Users.

Author	Study Period	Sample Source and Size	Self-Report/ Test	Serum/ Saliva	Sample Type and Size Tested	% Infected of Those Tested
Long *et al.*, (2000)	1999	Committal Prisoners[2] N=593	Test	Saliva	IDUs n=173	5.8
Allwright *et al.*, (1999)	1998	Irish Prison Population[3] N= 1,178	Test	Saliva	IDUs n=509	3.5
Smyth *et al.*, (1998)	1992 – 1997	Drug Treatment Centre N=735	Test	Serum	IDUs n=600	1.2
Dorman *et al.*, (1997)	1992	Drug Treatment Centre & Non-Treatment IDUs N=185	Test	Serum and Saliva	IDUs n=180	8.4
O'Kelly *et al.*, (1996)	1984 – 1995	IDUs in Community N=82	Test	Serum	IDUs n=66	65
Johnson *et al.*, (1994)	1991	Needle Exchange N=106	Test	Saliva	IDUs n=81	14.8

---

2   'Committal prisoners are prisoners who have been admitted to the prison within the preceding 48 hours, accused or guilty of a new crime, excluding those on temporary release or transferred from another prison. The committal population includes individuals entering on remand, following sentence, committed as a result of a bench warrant and non-nationals without valid documentation.' (Long *et al.*, 2000: 2).

3   All those incarcerated irrespective of their committal status.

In summary, injecting drug use continues to be one of the main risk categories to which HIV-positive cases are attributed each year. Despite the rates of new HIV-positive cases attributed to injecting drug use plateauing in the early and mid-1990s, recent figures suggest that there is an upward trend in the number of new HIV-positive cases among Irish drug users. The information available on those who are testing positive for HIV remains limited. Analysis of the figures highlights the need for more information, in particular of a socio-demographic and behavioural nature, to facilitate comprehensive epidemiological analysis of the trends.

Hepatitis B

There is very little information in Ireland on the prevalence and incidence of hepatitis B, among both the general population and the injecting drug-using population. While data are collected on the number of positive tests carried out for hepatitis B by the Virus Reference Laboratory, no behavioural data are collected and therefore those infected through drug use cannot be identified. Information on prevalence rates is therefore confined to a small number of special studies that have been carried out in the field (see Table 4.6).

TABLE 4.6

Ireland 1992–1999. Summary of Research Findings on the Prevalence of Hepatitis B Infection among Particular Cohorts of Drug Users.

Author	Study Period	Sample Source	Self-Report/ Test	Serum/ Saliva	Sample Type and Size Tested	% Infected of Those Tested
Long et al., (2000)	1999	Committal Prisoners N=593	Test	Saliva n=173	IDUs	17.9
Allwright et al., (1999)	1998	Irish Prison Population N=1,178	Test	Saliva n=509	IDUs	18.5
Smyth et al., (1998)	1992 – 1997	Drug Treatment Centre N=735	Test	Serum	IDUs n=729	1.0

Smyth, Keenan & O'Connor's (1998) study of drug users located within a treatment setting found that only 1 per cent were infected with hepatitis B. However, more recent research carried out in the prison setting found significantly higher prevalence rates among IDUs. Allwright, Barry, Bradley, Long & Thornton (1999) and Long, Allwright, Barry, Reaper-Reynolds, Thornton & Bradley (2000) found prevalence rates of 18.5 per cent and 17.9 per cent respectively for hepatitis B. While these figures suggest that hepatitis B may be prevalent among the injecting drug user population, the lack of data prohibits any in-depth epidemiological analysis of the situation in Ireland.

Hepatitis C

In Ireland, there are no routine data collected on hepatitis C. However, there have been a number of special studies carried out among samples of drug users in a variety of study settings (see Table 4.7). While it is not possible from the available data to analyse infection trends over time, it would appear that hepatitis C infection has been prevalent among Irish IDUs over the past decade. Hepatitis C prevalence rates among cohorts of treatment clients have been found to range from 52.1 per cent (Smyth, Keenan & O'Connor, 1999) up to 89 per cent (Smyth, McMahon, O'Connor & Ryan, 1999a).

TABLE 4.7
Ireland 1992–1999. Summary of Research Findings on the Prevalence of Hepatitis C Infection among Particular Cohorts of Drug Users.

Author	Study Period	Sample Source	Self-Report/ Test	Serum/ Saliva	Sample Type and Size Tested	% Infected of Those Tested
Long et al., (2000)	1999	Committal Prisoners N=593	Test	Serum	IDUs (n=173) Non IDUs (n=420)	IDUs 71.7 Non IDUs 1.4
Allwright et al., (1999)	1998	Irish Prison Population N= 1,178	Test	Serum	IDUs (n=509) Non IDUs (n=669)	IDUs 81.3 Non IDUs 3.7
Smyth et al., (1999)	1993 – 1996	Drug Treatment Centre N=353	Test	Serum	IDUs (n=353)	IDUs 52.1
Smyth et al., (1999a)	1997	Drug Treatment Centre N=84	Self- Report	NA	IDUs (n=84)	IDUs 89
Smyth et al., (1998)	1992– 1997	Drug Treatment Centre N=735	Test	Serum	IDUs (n=733)	IDUs 61.8
Smyth et al., (1995)	1992 – 1993	Drug Treatment Centre N=272	Test	Serum	IDUs (n=272)	IDUs 84

4.5 Other Drug-Related Morbidity

Psychiatric Co-Morbidity

A study to assess the differences between individuals who are (1) dependent on opiates and benzodiazepines, and (2) dependent on opiates, was carried out on patients consecutively admitted to a ten-bed inpatient drug-treatment unit in Dublin over a four-month period (Rooney, Kelly, Bamford, Sloan & O'Connor, 1999). More drug use and greater psychological morbidity were found among those dependent on opiates and benzodiazepines, than among those dependent on opiates. The former were more likely to describe a past experience of depression and a past episode of deliberate self-harm. However, despite this, none of them were regularly attending or obtaining treatment from a psychiatric service. This has implications for drug-treatment programmes, as continued benzodiazepine use leads to destabilisation of methadone maintenance programmes (Rooney *et al.*, 1999).

Williams, Mullan, O'Connor & Kinsella (1990) studied the level of depressive symptoms in a group of opiate users on methadone maintenance. All those attending the Drug Treatment Centre, Trinity Court, in Dublin, at the start of November 1988 were included in the study (N=70). All met the diagnostic criteria (DSM-3 – Diagnostic and Statistical Manual of Mental Disorders) for opiate dependence. Of the group, 83 per cent reported moderate or severe depressive symptoms. This finding cannot, however, be used in more wide-ranging conclusions because the study group was not representative of other populations of opiate-dependent users. The authors concluded that the relationship between depression and opiate dependency in the group was speculative and open to a number of interpretations. For example, opiate use may be a method of self-medication to relieve depressive feelings; or depressive symptoms could represent a reaction to problems of living, or could be explained by familial factors. The authors concluded that awareness and recognition of depressive symptoms were important elements in the effective treatment of opiate dependency.

Irish policy on the treatment of alcohol and drug misuse (Department of Health, 1984) stipulated that the emphasis in the management of alcohol and drug-related problems should be on community-based intervention, rather than on specialist inpatient treatment. Despite the general policy of providing treatment for problem drug use at non-residential services in the community, drug-related admissions to psychiatric inpatient hospitals are continuing to rise (see Table 3.3 at Appendix 3). The proportion of drug-related admissions, with a primary or secondary diagnosis, increased from 2.2 per cent in 1995 to 3.6 per cent in 1999 for all admissions (information obtained from the National Psychiatric Inpatient Reporting System (NPIRS), maintained in the Mental Health

Division of the HRB). For first admissions (admission for the first time ever), the proportion increased from 2.4 per cent to 5 per cent in the same period. This is in contrast to the general trend of a decrease in overall admissions to psychiatric hospitals.

The rates (per 100,000 population) of all admissions to psychiatric hospitals increased from 16.2 in 1995 to 24.6 in 1999, and in the case of first admissions the rate doubled between 1995 and 1999, from 4.7 to 9.8 per 100,000 population. Admission rates for 'drug dependence' to inpatient psychiatric hospitals vary according to geographic location (see Table 4.8). This is not necessarily an indication of morbidity but may perhaps be linked to drug-treatment provision in different areas and/or more willingness in certain areas to admit people with drug problems to psychiatric hospitals.

TABLE 4.8

Ireland 1997–1999. First Admissions to Inpatient Psychiatric Hospitals, with Drug Dependence Diagnosis, by Hospital Board Area. Rates per 100,000 Population, Aged 16 Years and Over.

Health Board Area	1997	1998	1999
Eastern	10.9	13.4	13.4
Midland	10.1	8.0	17.4
Mid-Western	10.6	10.2	13.2
North-Eastern	6.3	6.8	8.6
North-Western	6.5	6.5	2.6
South-Eastern	7.1	8.0	8.7
Southern	6.6	6.1	6.1
Western	5.4	6.5	7.7
Total	**8.7**	**9.6**	**10.6**

Source: NPIRS, Mental Health Division, HRB.

The NPIRS data from 1997 to 1999 did not show any noteworthy psychiatric co-morbidity. To some extent close family ties and good family supports could have been a factor in preventing people with psychiatric disorders from becoming involved in problematic drug use. However, it might also indicate that drug-dependent people with psychiatric co-morbidity were not obtaining treatment from psychiatric services, as was found in the Rooney *et al.* (1999) study.

Another topic that has been receiving some attention recently is the possible association between drug misuse and attention deficit hyperactivity disorder (ADHD). In an attempt to draw attention to the concerns of the Irish Council of Attention Deficit Disorder Support Groups, a submission was made on their behalf to the National Drugs Strategy Review, which took place during 2000. The submission was made as a result of concern that ADHD may be a significant risk factor leading to involvement in substance misuse, and that people with ADHD are more likely to self-medicate. The aim was to highlight the need to identify drug users who suffer from ADHD and to ensure the provision of appropriate treatment programmes for their care and management.

Other Health Issues

The Medical Bureau of Road Safety, Department of Forensic Medicine, National University of Ireland (NUI), Dublin, in collaboration with An Garda Síochána, has undertaken a study to determine current trends in driving under the influence of drugs in Ireland (Moane, Leavy & Cusack, 2000). The survey will investigate the presence of amphetamines, benzodiazepines, cannabis, cocaine, opiates and methadone in blood and urine samples taken by the Gardaí under the Road Traffic Act, 1994. One thousand samples will be randomly selected, as well as another 1,000 from those under the legal alcohol limit for driving. Preliminary results (see Table 4.9) from 338 samples (under the legal alcohol limit) showed that cannabis was most frequently found (34%), followed by benzodiazepines (25%). Cocaine was the drug least commonly found (4%) (Moane *et al.*, 2000). These results indicate that there has been a significant increase in driving under the influence of drugs since 1987, when a similar study was carried out and 14.6 per cent of samples (under the legal alcohol limit) tested positive for drugs. The current preliminary study found that the percentage had risen to 37 per cent. The results of this survey will identify the types of drugs being taken and their combination with other drugs, including alcohol.

TABLE 4.9.

Drugs Driving in Ireland 2000. Preliminary Study of Prevalence of Driving under the Influence of Drugs – for Sample under Legal Alcohol Limit. Type of Drug. Percentages.

Type of Drug	Driving under Influence of Drug (under Legal Alcohol Limit) (%)
Cannabis	34
Benzodiazepines	25
Amphetamines	16
Opiates	14
Methadone	7
Cocaine	4

Source: Moane *et al.*, 2000.

4.6 Drug-Related Mortality

Official Irish statistics on drug-related deaths from the General Mortality Register (GMR) are compiled routinely by the Central Statistics Office (CSO). They are coded according to the International Classification of Diseases, Version 9 (ICD–9), that is, the cause of death is designated as the underlying cause of death. This is defined as:

> … (a) the disease or injury which initiated the train of morbid events leading directly to death, or (b) the circumstances of the accident or violence which produced the fatal injury. (WHO, 1977: 700)

The underlying cause of death can be from natural or external causes. The definition of external cause of death is as follows:

> … a supplementary classification that may be used, if desired, to code external factors associated with morbid conditions classified to any part of the main classifications. For single-cause tabulation of the underlying cause of death, however, the E Code should be used as a primary code if, and only if, the morbid condition is classifiable to Injury and Poisoning. (WHO, 1977: xxix)

For the purpose of this report a drug-related death is defined as one where the underlying (natural or external) cause of death was drug dependence (ICD-9, Code 304) or opiate poisoning (ICD-9, Code 965.0). These are deaths directly related to problem drug use.

An examination of drug-related deaths recorded between 1990 and 1999 (see Table 3.1 at Appendix 3) shows that the number of deaths over the ten-year period increased considerably from 1995 onwards. The highest number was recorded (N=99) in 1998. It was during that time that amendments were made to the information recorded by An Garda Síochána for the CSO; this was as a result of the work of the National Task Force on Suicide (Department of Health, 1996, and Department of Health and Children, 1998). In the case of a sudden or suspicious death, a member of An Garda Síochána attends the scene of death and subsequently completes a data form (Form 104) for the CSO. The amendment relevant to the recording of a drug-related death consists of a question on drug/alcohol dependency. This obviously had an effect on the statistics recorded subsequently. The increase in the number of deaths, as recorded by the GMR between 1990 and 1999, was thus partly due to greater awareness of the need for such information, and the consequent improvement in the collection procedure of the GMR data, and partly due to a real increase in the number of drug-related deaths.

The increasing trend did not continue in 1999, when the number of deaths was eighty (see Table 3.1 at Appendix 3). In terms of geographic location the vast majority of deaths were in Dublin, where the opiate problem is mainly concentrated. The majority were males, between the ages of 15 and 49.

Indirect as well as direct drug-related death was the subject of an *ad hoc* retrospective study carried out by Keating, Ramsbottom & Harbison (1999). Dublin City and County coroners' files were examined to study the number of drug-related (direct and indirect) deaths in 1997. The criteria for inclusion were that the death:

- had occurred in Dublin (city or county) between 1 January and 31 December 1997;
- had positive toxicological evidence of the presence of drugs; and
- had drugs implicated in the cause of death.

This is a much broader definition than that used for the purpose of the GMR. Toxicological screens included testing for alcohol, opiates, benzodiazepines, tricyclics, barbiturates and cocaine. It was found that 120 cases were toxicologically positive for drugs, and 65 of these were known to be drug users. The gender ratio was 3:1 (male:female) and more than half of the deaths were in the 20- to 39-year-old age group. The drug most commonly identified was benzodiazepine (seventy-five cases), mainly in combination with other drugs. The most common combination of drugs was opiates and benzodiazepines. Methadone was found in forty-seven cases; alcohol in forty-seven cases; heroin in twenty-seven cases; tricyclics in twenty-one cases; cannabis in fifteen cases; phenothiazines in twelve cases; opiates in twelve cases; paracetamol in twelve cases; cocaine in seven cases; barbiturates in four cases; MDMA in two cases; amphetamines in two cases; and butane in two cases. A similar study of coroners' files in 1992 (in Keating *et al.*, 1999) found no cocaine, MDMA or amphetamines in drug-related deaths. The 1992 study found a similar number of drug-related deaths recorded (in Dublin coroners' files) to that recorded in the GMR for that year. However, the total number (N=120) found in the 1997 study did not correspond with the total number (N=49) recorded in the more narrowly-defined GMR for the same year.

In summer 2000, an outbreak of twenty-four cases of illness among IDUs in the Dublin area resulted in eight deaths. This was similar to an outbreak of the same illness in Glasgow, where the first cases were recognised. While the definitive cause of death for all cases has not yet been established, the likely cause has been identified as a toxin-producing strain of *Clostridium novyi*, but other bacteria may have been involved. The 'significance of the presence of clostridial species remains to be determined but it may suggest contamination of the drugs or other materials' used by the IDUs (Andraghetti *et al.*, 2000).

4.7 Summary

Over 70 per cent of those presenting for treatment for the first time are under 25 years old. This is younger than in other EU countries and is a reflection of the demography of Ireland, where nearly half the population (48%) is under 30 years of age (see Table 2.1 at Appendix 2). The profile of the typical drug user receiving treatment is young, unemployed male, leaving school at an early age, and living in a socially and economically disadvantaged area. However, there were some positive developments towards the end of the 1990s. There was a decrease in the number leaving school before the age of 16 years, and there was a sizeable increase in the level of employment among problem drug users. These trends reflected more general changes in Irish society, related to improvements in the economy over the same period.

There is great disparity in the pattern of drug use in different parts of the country. Problematic opiate/heroin use occurs mainly in the eastern region of the country, around Dublin. In other areas, cannabis is the drug for which the majority of people receive treatment. Heroin users are much less likely to be still at school than cannabis users, and they are much more likely to be involved in behaviours detrimental to their health, such as injecting, and sharing injecting equipment.

Trends in patterns of drug use have been changing since the beginning of the 1990s. Between 1990 and 1996, among those presenting for treatment for the first time, there was a trend towards smoking, rather than injecting, heroin. Smoking seems to have been the preferred route for young people starting to use heroin, at least in the initial year or so of their drug-using careers. However, trends since 1997 show that this has changed. The explanation is likely to be a complex one, involving many factors such as the perceptions of drug users, the availability of heroin, and fluctuations in the price of heroin. But it may be that young people, who initially preferred to smoke, become more willing to inject once heroin use had become habitual.

Trends in high-risk behaviours over the time period 1990 – 1997 have shown a significant decrease – needle-sharing practices have fallen and safe sex practices (use of condoms) have increased. This could be attributed to the increase in the services provided for people involved in risky drug-related behaviours, including the availability of clean injecting equipment. However, women were found to be more at risk than men, but, while women tend to be involved in more risky behaviours than male drug users, they present earlier for treatment than men. Young IDUs were found to be a particularly at-risk group.

The most comprehensive data available on drug-related infectious diseases in Ireland are for HIV. While the number of new positive-tested cases for HIV, which were attributable to injecting drug use, appeared to stabilise in the mid-1990s, figures for 1999 show an increase in the number of cases. For both hepatitis B and hepatitis C, analysis is dependent solely on data from special studies. Despite the absence of comprehensive data, it appears from the evidence available that hepatitis C continues to be highly prevalent among Irish IDUs. Overall, it would appear that drug-related infectious diseases continue to be an issue of concern in relation to IDUs. This highlights the need for more comprehensive data collection in the area of all drug-related infectious diseases, in order to monitor changes in the trends over time.

4.8 References

Allwright, S., Barry, J., Bradley, F., Long, J. & Thornton, L. (1999). *Hepatitis B, Hepatitis C and HIV in Irish Prisoners: Prevalence and risk.* Dublin: The Stationery Office.

Andraghetti, R., Goldberg, D., Smith, A., O'Flanagan, D., Lieftucht, A. & Gill, N. (2000). Update: Illness among injecting drug users in Scotland, Ireland and England. *EPI-INSIGHT, 1,* 4, September 2000.

Cassin, S., Geoghegan, T. & Cox, G. (1998). Young injectors: A comparative analysis of risk behaviour. *Irish Journal of Medical Science, 167,* (4), 234–237.

Department of Health (1984). *The Psychiatric Services – Planning for the future.* Dublin: The Stationery Office.

Department of Health (1996). *National Task Force on Suicide – Interim report.* Dublin: The Stationery Office.

Department of Health and Children (1998). *Report of the National Task Force on Suicide.* Dublin: The Stationery Office.

Dillon, L. (forthcoming). *Drug Use among Prisoners: An exploratory study.* Dublin: The Health Research Board.

Dorman, A., Keenan, E., Schuttler, C., Merry, J. & O'Connor, J. (1997). HIV risk behaviour in Irish intravenous drug users. *Irish Journal of Medicine, 166,* (4), 235–238.

Geoghegan, T., O'Shea, M. & Cox, G. (1999). Gender differences in characteristics of drug users presenting to a Dublin syringe exchange. *Irish Journal Psychological Medicine, 16,* (4), 131–135.

Johnson, Z., O'Connor, M., Pomeroy, L., Johnson, H., Barry, J., Scully, M. & Fitzpatrick, E. (1994). Prevalence of HIV and associated risk behaviour in attendees at a Dublin needle exchange. *Addiction, 89,* 603–607.

Keating, C., Ramsbottom, V. & Harbison, J. (1999). 'An Analysis of Drug-Related Deaths in Dublin City and County in 1997'. Unpublished.

Long, J., Allwright, S., Barry, J., Reaper-Reynolds, S., Thornton, L. & Bradley, F. (2000). *Hepatitis B, Hepatitis C and HIV in Irish Prisoners, Part II: Prevalence and risk in committal prisoners 1999.* Dublin: The Stationery Office.

Moane, S., Leavy, C. P. & Cusack, D. A. (2000). *Drugs Driving in Ireland – A preliminary study of the prevalence of driving under the influence of drugs on Irish roads.* Dublin: Medical Bureau of Road Safety, Department of Forensic Medicine, University College, Dublin.

Moran, R., O'Brien, M. & Duff, P. (1997). *Treated Drug Misuse in Ireland. National report 1996.* Dublin: The Health Research Board.

Mullen, L. & Barry, J. (1999). *Needle Exchange in the Eastern Health Board Region: An analysis of first attenders 1990 – 1997.* Dublin: Eastern Health Board.

O'Brien, M., Moran, R., Kelleher, T. & Cahill, P. (2000). *National Drug Treatment Reporting System. Statistical bulletin 1997 and 1998.* Dublin: The Health Research Board.

O'Kelly, F. & Bury, G. (1996). An analysis of the effects of HIV infection in a cohort of intravenous drug users. *Irish Medical Journal, 89,* (3), 112–114.

O'Neill, M. & O'Connor, A. M. (1999). *Drug-Using Women Working in Prostitution.* Dublin: The Women's Health Project, Eastern Health Board.

Rooney, S., Kelly, G., Bamford, L., Sloan, D. & O'Connor, J. J. (1999). Co-abuse of opiates and benzodiazepines. *Irish Journal Medical Science, 168,* (1), 37– 41.

Smyth, R., Keenan, E., Dorman, A. & O'Connor, J. (1995). Hepatitis C infection among injecting drug users attending the National Drug Treatment Centre. *Irish Journal of Medical Science, 164*, (6), 267–268.

Smyth, B., Keenan, E. & O'Connor, J. (1998). Bloodborne viral infection in Irish injecting drug users. *Addiction, 93*, (11), 1649–1656.

Smyth, B., Keenan, E. & O'Connor, J. (1999). Evaluation of the impact of Dublin's expanded harm reduction programme on prevalence of hepatitis C among short-term injecting drug users. *Journal of Epidemiology and Community Health, 53*, (7), 434– 435.

Smyth, B., McMahon, J., O'Connor, J. & Ryan, J. (1999a). Knowledge regarding hepatitis C among injecting drug users. *Drugs: Education, Prevention and Policy, 6*, (2), 257–264.

Smyth, B., McMahon, J. O'Connor, J. & Ryan, J. (1999b). The use of primary care services by opiate-dependent injecting drug users in the era of 'shared care'. *European Journal of General Practice, 5*, 143–148.

Smyth, B., O'Brien, M. & Barry, J. (2000). Trends in treated opiate misuse in Dublin: the emergence of chasing the dragon. *Addiction, 95*, 8, 1217–1223.

WHO (1977). *Manual of the International Statistical Classification of Diseases, Injuries and Causes of Death, Volume 1.* Geneva: World Health Organisation.

Williams, H., Mullan, E., O'Connor, J. & Kinsella, A. (1990). Risk behaviour for HIV transmission in attenders on methadone maintenance. *Irish Journal of Medical Science, 159*, (5), 141–144.

CHAPTER 5

SOCIAL ISSUES AND PUBLIC ATTITUDES ASSOCIATED WITH DRUG MISUSE

PAULA MAYOCK AND ROSALYN MORAN

5.1 Introduction

Little research in the Irish context has examined social and environmental issues relating to drug misuse,[1] despite consistent findings from the national epidemiological database on drug misuse, the National Drug Treatment Reporting System (NDTRS), which indicates high rates of social deprivation among treated drug users (O'Hare & O'Brien, 1992; O'Higgins, 1996; Moran, O'Brien & Duff, 1997).

This chapter briefly reviews recent literature relevant to drug use and aspects of social exclusion in Ireland. Secondly, general public attitudes to drug use and drug users are considered in light of recent research pertaining to drug-related attitudes among the general population. Finally, the chapter highlights a number of drug-related issues that have emerged in the public domain in recent years.

5.2 Drug Use, Housing and Homelessness

For several years professionals working in disadvantaged communities and in the field of drug treatment have been aware that the development of long-term and damaging drug

---

[1] The National Advisory Committee on Drugs (NACD) has called for tenders for a number of overviews of available literature on social aspects of drug misuse.

use is most often associated with social marginalisation and exclusion (McCarthy & McCarthy, 1995; Loughran, 1996). Over the past two decades research in Ireland has consistently demonstrated a link between concentrations of drug use and various indicators of poverty and social exclusion, including unemployment, poor housing, one-parent families and low educational attainment (Dean, Bradshaw & Lavelle, 1983; O'Kelly, Bury, Cullen & Dean, 1988; McKeown, Fitzgerald & Deegan, 1993; O'Higgins & O'Brien, 1995; Coveney, Murphy-Lawless, Redmond & Sheridan, 1999). In 1996 Irish Government drug policy recognised the link between poverty and concentrations of serious drug problems in the *First Report of the Ministerial Task Force on Measures to Reduce the Demand for Drugs* (Ministerial Task Force, 1996*)*. This report signalled the first official recognition of the role of environmental or contextual factors in the development of drug-related problems (Butler, 1997). The Irish National Drugs Strategy, which aims to provide an integrated response to the problems posed by drug misuse, can be characterised as supporting general initiatives to tackle social exclusion and specific initiatives targeted at drug-related problems (see Chapter 1).

The opiate epidemic of the 1980s was followed by a period of relative stability in heroin uptake rates (Dean, O'Hare, O'Connor, Melly & Kelly, 1987). However, by the mid-1990s, suggestions of a 'new' wave of young heroin users had emerged (O'Gorman, 1998) and this coincided with renewed attention to the plight of families, parents and children living in neighbourhoods with high concentrations of drug use. Public awareness of drug use and related criminal activities increased quite dramatically around this time, a development that appears to have been prompted by a number of factors. According to O'Donnell (1999), reports of a near doubling in the number of murders between 1994 and 1995 contributed to public anxiety about violent crime, as did extensive media coverage of the lavish lifestyles of key perpetrators of organised crime. This situation intensified during 1996, when community members in a number of Dublin city areas mobilised and engaged in direct action, marching on the homes of suspected drug dealers, with the intention of 'cleaning' their communities of drug 'pushers'. Media attention on the activities of resident anti-drug and vigilante groups intensified, raising public awareness of drug-related activities as well as the link between drug use and crime. The murders of Garda Detective Gerry McCabe and journalist Veronica Guerin in 1996, which resulted in public outrage and heightened intolerance of drug-related activities, forced the drugs issue to the top of the political agenda (Memery & Kerrins, 2000).

In December 1996 the Government introduced the Housing (Miscellaneous Provisions) Bill, which was enacted in July 1997. This legislation was one of several measures taken to strengthen and extend the existing statutory framework for the control of drugs (Loughran, 1999). The aim of the legislation was to enable local authorities to evict individuals believed to be engaged in anti-social behaviour (Silke, 1999). According to Sections (1) (a) and (1) (b) of the 1997 Act, anti-social behaviour includes either or both of the following:

(a) the manufacture, production, preparation, importation, exportation, sale or supply, possession for the purposes of sale or supply, or distribution of a controlled drug (within the meaning of the Misuse of Drugs Act, 1977 and 1984);

(b) any behaviour which causes or is likely to cause any significant or persistent danger, injury, damage, loss or fear to any person living, working or otherwise lawfully in or in the vicinity of a house provided by a housing authority under the Housing Acts, 1966 to 1997, or a housing estate in which the house is situated and, without prejudice to the foregoing, includes violence, threats, intimidation, coercion, harassment or serious obstruction of any person.

Kelly (1997) expressed concern about the legislation before it was passed, warning that it was likely to increase homelessness, and was particularly critical of the 'loose' definition of 'anti-social behaviour'. The legislation was, and remains, strongly criticised by several sectors involved in the care and rehabilitation of drug users. However, it was equally strongly supported and welcomed by certain community activists.

According to the Merchant's Quay Project, a voluntary service providing a range of services to drug users seeking help, the Housing Act, 1997, has contributed to an increase in the number of homeless drug users in Dublin (Memery et al., 2000). In its recently-published annual report, the Merchant's Quay Project has recorded an increase in the number of young drug users sleeping rough and has claimed that 'both homelessness and lack of experience of drug use make these drug users a particularly vulnerable group in terms of risk of infection and general health and well being' (Merchant's Quay Project, 2000: 1). A recent analysis of Dublin Simon's outreach contacts has similarly highlighted drug use as a major difficulty among the total contact group presenting to the Simon Community. Its 1999 figures indicate that 25 per cent of male, and 32 per cent of female, contacts presented with drug problems (Howley, 2000).

Research undertaken by Cox & Lawless (1999) on homeless drug users in Dublin City exemplifies the extreme vulnerability of this group. The researchers found that, among the group, there were low levels of educational attainment, high unemployment and histories of serving prison sentences. Fifty-six per cent of the study's respondents reported that their drug use had escalated as a result of being out of home. In addition, homeless drug users were found to engage in very high levels of risk behaviour, with 66 per cent of clients injecting in public places, 49 per cent reporting sharing injecting equipment and a further 24 per cent stating that they had recently borrowed used injecting equipment. Moreover, the authors argued that the difficulties confronting this highly-marginalised group were further exacerbated by their exclusion from some of the homeless services, owing to a policy of non-acceptance of active drug users in most direct access accommodation such as hostels and shelters. In a small-scale qualitative study of fifteen homeless drug users, Costello & Howley (2000) also noted the numerous negative consequences of excluding drug users from accommodation services for homeless people, including increased likelihood of sharing needles, lack of safe places to store and dispose of needles, lack of access to clean injecting equipment, and the lack of a clean, safe environment in which to inject. Furthermore, several of their respondents perceived the Housing Act, 1997, as leading to their exclusion from opportunities to gain access to independent housing. The respondents' perception that they were discriminated against by local authorities and residents' committees, because of their drug use, was reported as creating a considerable barrier to their seeking accommodation. Similarly, Woods (2000), reporting on a study of female drug users' experience of parenting, found that respondents described the Housing Act, 1997, as 'anti-woman' and 'anti-family' (Woods, 2000: 279). Several women recounted cases where drug users had been delivered the ultimatum to either access treatment or leave their communities. Drugs workers interviewed for the purpose of the research also expressed anger at this situation, which they regarded as an additional exclusionary measure against extremely vulnerable individuals.

The impact of the Housing (Miscellaneous Provisions) Act, 1997, has recently been assessed by Memery et al. (2000). Their report documented an increase in evictions related to anti-social behaviour by Dublin Corporation since the introduction of the Housing Act, 1997. The authors concluded:

> Instead of working to resolve the wider and complex drug issues for these communities and address the needs of drug users directly, a very blunt piece of legislation was put in place with the emphasis on excluding those involved with drugs from local authority housing (Memery et al., 2000: 29).

Official documentation from supporters of the Housing Act, 1997, is more difficult to assess as community and local newspapers tend to be the source for such articles. Moreover, the focus of extant research on this legislation has been on the experiences of drug users themselves rather than on community members not involved in drug use. Anecdotal evidence suggests, however, that there are pockets of support for the legislation.

There is scope for more research into, and open documentation of, drug-related issues in general, and for making 'grey' literature in the drugs area more accessible. The new National Documentation Centre on Drugs, which is being established in the Drug Misuse Research Division (DMRD) of the Health Research Board (HRB), aims to provide a focus for such 'grey' literature.

5.3. Public Nuisance and Community Problems

There is relatively little research in the Irish context into living conditions and quality of life in communities where drug problems exist. However, a recent study of social housing across seven local authority estates in urban areas throughout Ireland (Fahey, 1999) highlighted a range of problems in the estates studied.

Reporting on the social order problems identified by residents, O'Higgins (1999) noted that the nature of the problems experienced across the seven estates varied. At one end of the scale, social problems consisted of relatively minor 'nuisance behaviour', while at the other end, a number of estates endured more serious problems, ranging from illegal drug use and dealing to intimidation and harassment. The findings indicated that the use of heroin and other 'hard' drugs was confined mainly to Dublin estates, and was particularly acute in one large local-authority flat complex located in Dublin's south inner city. The profound negative effects of concentrations of drug problems emerged strongly from the reports of children living in the estate, who were interviewed as part of the research. Children in focus groups recounted routine encounters with drug users and made casual reference to the presence of drugs paraphernalia on the stairs, on balconies and in the stairwells. Coupled with this, parents expressed extreme anxiety about the negative consequences of high levels of drug exposure for their children. Drug use and activities related to the distribution of illegal drugs were considered to impact negatively on the quality of life of a high proportion of residents and to be among the most enduring problems on the estate.

Corcoran (1998), reporting on research carried out in one large local authority housing complex in inner-city Dublin, found that all aspects of the drug problem, including drug-taking in public areas and the sale and distribution of drugs, were perceived as extremely problematic. Both Corcoran (1998) and O'Higgins (1999) noted that the activities surrounding the distribution of drugs drew a steady stream of non-residents onto this estate. This, among other factors, exacerbated the 'palpable sense of tension' (Corcoran, 1998: 21) in the area. Furthermore, there was a widespread belief among residents that the drug situation was out of the control of both residents and the Gardaí (McAuliffe & Fahey, 1999).

Morley (1998), in a study carried out in another inner-city flat complex with a long history of social problems, also highlighted the perceived negative impact of drug problems on the quality of life in the community. The socio-economic profile of the estate revealed in the research – high rates of long-term unemployment, low educational attainment levels and high rates of early school leaving – was again indicative of a community struggling with the issues of social exclusion and marginalisation. This estate also hosted a large number of problem opiate users.

The management of social order problems on local authority estates has involved, *inter alia*, evictions of problem tenants, particularly those individuals associated with drug dealing and related activities. Fahey (1999) concluded that, while the use of exclusionary strategies has resulted in some improvements in social order in a number of estates, such policies ultimately exacerbate social exclusion and result in further social problems. In recent years, more participatory approaches to estate management have been introduced and include communication and consultation with tenants in the planning, development and revitalisation of estates (Fahey, 1999; O'Gorman, 2000). There is a need for greater innovation and experimentation with different models of estate management, particularly in environments where drug problems exist.

5.4 Social and Economic Costs of Drug Consumption

Studies or estimates of the healthcare and other social costs of drug consumption have not been carried out in Ireland; neither have the economic costs to society from drug use been researched.

Accepting that the 'social costs' incurred through drug use can be defined and interpreted variously, and that no research has been undertaken in Ireland with the specific aim of estimating such costs, a number of research findings may be drawn on as indicative of significant costs to individuals, families and communities as a result of drug use.

As might be expected, this evidence arises primarily from research on a range of social problems associated mainly with disadvantaged communities. The previous section overviewed recent studies illustrating the perceived negative impact of high levels of drug misuse on communities where drug use is concentrated (Morley, 1998; Corcoran, 1998; O'Higgins, 1999). Residents of such communities consistently draw attention to the destructive effect of drug use and drug trafficking on community life. Furthermore, they are acutely aware of the negative way in which outsiders perceive their community. Mayock (2000), in a qualitative study of drug use by young people in a Dublin inner-city community, similarly noted that respondents made constant reference to the area's drug problem. Furthermore, the young people expressed strong resentment of outside representations of their neighbourhood and were particularly critical of the negative effects of disparaging media reports on their community. Many clearly felt stigmatised by virtue of living in a locality where drug use and associated activities were concentrated.

There is relatively little research available pertaining to the consequences of drug problems for individual families.[2] For example, there is no estimate of the number of individuals affected by familial drug use. However, the issue of how children are affected by drug misuse has emerged as an issue of critical concern. Hogan (1997) undertook an exploratory study of the social and psychological needs of children of drug-using parents, based on interviews with key workers, teachers and carers. This study identified factors which place children of drug users 'at risk for inadequate care and for psychological difficulties' (Hogan, 1997: 36). Information attained on the school experiences of six children indicated that teachers rated half (n=3) as poor attenders and half as falling behind their age level in reading and mathematics. Key workers interviewed for the purpose of the research expressed concern about the quality and consistency of care giving by drug-using parents. However, parents who were receiving treatment for their drug problems appeared less likely to experience parenting difficulties and many were perceived to be coping competently with child rearing. Woods (2000) noted that professional workers in the drug treatment and social work fields are generally positive about women drug users and their involvement with their children. The absence of childcare facilities offered to drug-using women was identified as presenting a significant barrier to mothers' participation in further education and in the workforce. This finding also emerged from Moran's (1999) study of the availability, use and provision of crèche facilities in drug-treatment contexts.

The need for an integrated approach to services aimed at drug-using parents and their children was acknowledged in the *First Report of the Ministerial Task Force on Measures to Reduce the Demand for Drugs* (Ministerial Task Force, 1996). The Eastern Health Board's *Review of Adequacy* (1997) identified the key issues for these families as 'addiction, child care, health (physical and emotional), housing, criminality and employment' (Eastern Health Board, 1997: 51). Increased recognition of the special needs of such families led to the setting-up of a specialised service providing intensive support to families where a parent(s) has a chronic opiate problem. A recent evaluation of this community drugs service revealed positive outcomes for both parents and children (Murphy & Hogan, 1999). Reporting on parents' perceptions of the service, the authors noted that parents

---

2   The National Advisory Committee on Drugs (NACD) has commissioned a study to overview literature in this and related areas. Results are expected mid-2001.

particularly valued a social work approach, which acknowledged their needs both as parents and as individuals and where the emphasis was not exclusively on the care and monitoring of their children.

5.5 Developments in Public Attitudes and Debates

This section overviews empirical findings regarding public attitudes to drug-related issues. This is followed by an account of some drug-related issues, which have been the subject of political and public debate in recent times (i.e. during 2000). The intent of the latter is to provide a flavour of the types of issues currently being discussed in the public domain.

The first national survey of drug-related knowledge, attitudes and beliefs in Ireland, known as the KAB1 study, was published by the DMRD of the HRB in September 2000 (Bryan, Moran, Farrell & O'Brien, 2000). The questionnaire on which the research was based[3] constituted a module of the 1998 Irish Social Omnibus Survey. A total of 1,000 adults aged 18 years and older, randomly selected from the 1997 Register of Electors for Ireland, took part in the study. Data were collected using face-to-face interviews between February and April 1998. An expanded study, KAB2, was carried out in early 2001 and results from the study will be published by the DMRD of the HRB towards the end of 2001.[4]

The main findings from KAB1 are summarised as follows:

- Members of the general public were generally aware of the kinds of illegal drugs most commonly used. Ninety-four per cent reported that they had heard of heroin, cocaine, ecstasy and cannabis, while 70 per cent had heard of LSD and amphetamines.
- Self-reported cannabis use (as measured by lifetime prevalence) stood at 12 per cent for the entire sample. The younger urban sector of society tended to have greater personal experience of cannabis and to know people who had taken cannabis or had 'a drug problem'. Males reported greater use of cannabis and knowledge of cannabis users than females.

---

3   Based on Moran (1977).

4   The study explores respondents' approval / disapproval of people taking different types of drugs; perceived harm / risk associated with different substances; whether respondents had ever been offered drugs, by whom, and in what environment; the ease with which respondents could access drugs; and source of first drug used. KAB2 will allow exploration of methodological issues, e.g. reliability, etc., and has been designed to provide information regarding the reliability of findings from the Kelleher (forthcoming) study and to provide comparative information with data from Northern Ireland samples.

- The results indicated a high level of concern about the current drug situation among the general public.
- A substantial proportion of respondents believed that experimentation with drugs was commonplace among young people. Over half of those who took part in the survey believed that it was 'normal' for young people to try drugs at least once, and at least 40 per cent believed that most young people experimented with cannabis and ecstasy.
- Respondents generally regarded illegal drug taking as a dangerous pursuit. Approximately three-quarters (77%) believed all illegal drugs to be equally harmful to health, while over 40 per cent believed that one could become dependent on drugs after just one experience. Half the sample (54%) believed regular use of cannabis was just as dangerous to health as regular use of heroin. This somewhat exaggerated sense of the effects of illegal drugs was less common among the younger members of the adult population surveyed.
- Social avoidance and fear of drug users and those addicted to drugs were high among respondents. Moreover, sympathy for drug-addicted individuals was relatively low. Younger respondents and respondents with a higher level of education were less inclined to perceive drug addicts in a negative light. Moreover, those with personal knowledge of someone 'with a drug problem' typically held more positive attitudes towards those who were addicted to drugs.
- Consistent with the widespread concern about the severity of the current drug situation was an overwhelmingly high level of support for drug prevention. Over 90 per cent of respondents agreed that the allocation of financial resources for drug prevention was worthwhile. Almost 95 per cent supported the notion of providing drug education to primary school children.
- Current harm reduction initiatives, including the provision of heroin substitutes such as methadone, and needle exchange facilities to heroin dependent clients, received support from two-thirds of respondents (63% and 66% respectively). Furthermore, while the provision of drug treatment on the basis of need received almost unanimous support, two-thirds of respondents (65%) felt this should only be provided to those who had abstinence as their ultimate goal.
- Regarding alternative policy options, 76 per cent of respondents agreed that cannabis use should be against the law, while over 70 per cent agreed that drug addicts convicted of petty offences should be given the option of receiving treatment instead of having a jail sentence for their crime.

The authors summarised the main findings and associated recommendations as follows:

Information about Drugs

Finding – The Irish have a good general awareness of commonly-used illegal drugs. However, their perception of the general harmfulness of these substances indicates a lack of accurate knowledge about the different effects associated with different types of drugs.

Recommendation – The provision of accurate information, of a non-sensationalist type, to all age groups, on the relative known risks associated with different types of drugs.

Societal Attitudes towards Drug Users

Finding – Societal attitudes towards drug users are mostly negative. Those with personal experience of someone 'with a drug problem' tend to have less negative attitudes, as do the younger adults surveyed and those with higher levels of education.

Recommendation – The promotion of more positive attitudes towards those who misuse drugs, particularly among older people and those with less education. A positive attitudinal climate is important to the social integration of problem drug users and to their willingness to avail of treatment.

Concern about Legal as well as Illegal Drugs

Finding – The public generally perceives drug taking to be common among young people, and there is a high level of concern about the current drug situation in Ireland. Notwithstanding this, alcohol abuse tends to be perceived as a more serious problem in society than drug abuse.

Recommendation – The continuation of efforts to address the problem of legal as well as illegal drugs.

Drug Problem regarded as Very Serious Issue

Finding – While societal attitudes towards those who use drugs are negative, respondents attach high priority to providing help to drug users. This high level of support for drug treatment is likely to be related to the widespread perception that the drug problem is a very serious issue in Irish society.

Recommendation – The retention of the drugs issue high on the political and social agenda.

In general, issues surrounding the misuse of drugs, and the associated public debate, receive a high level of attention in the media. Law enforcement issues receiving media attention include policing initiatives, drug seizures, drug-related crime, criminal law cases, and the lifestyles of drug 'barons'. In addition, one of the issues frequently reported on is the opposition of local communities to the opening of drug-treatment facilities in their neighbourhoods – the NIMBY phenomenon (Not In My Back Yard). In response to such opposition, health boards endeavour to involve local communities in the planning of services. More recently, the outbreak of illness and deaths among injecting drug users (IDUs) in Dublin during 2000 received a lot of media coverage, which, *inter alia*, reiterated the risks taken by drug users.

A further area, which has received a high level of media attention, is the exploratory methodological work carried out by Comiskey (1998) on estimation of prevalence of opiate use in Dublin. Comiskey concluded from her work that estimates for opiate users in Dublin 'ranged from over 6,000 among medical data sources up to approximately 14,000 among the three data sources.' (Comiskey, 1998: 1). The three data sources were the Central Patient Methadone Treatment List, the Hospital Inpatient Enquiry Database (HIPE), and records of Garda arrests, charges or suspected criminal activities (see Section 6.7). The three-data-source approach was based on a capture-recapture methodology. Uhl (2000), in a detailed technical paper, concluded that 'for the time being one has to warn seriously against regarding capture-recapture estimates as reliable, scientifically-based estimates. As we could demonstrate: the true number may easily be 50% less or 100% more than estimated' (Uhl, 2000: 2). The fact that the Dublin results are estimates is rarely noted in media reports, and rarer still is the presentation of ranges and confidence intervals or a number of estimates, as recommended by the European Monitoring Centre for Drugs and Drug Addiction (EMCDDA, 1997). As a consequence, in general media coverage has not been very balanced.

The DMRD is working with a National Working Group on Prevalence to improve the data available for such prevalence estimation. The first meeting of this group (DMRD, 2000) adopted, *inter alia*, a set of recommendations aimed at improving standards in the conduct and reporting of prevalence data (see Appendix 1).

In 2000, two issues, prescription of heroin and decriminalisation of cannabis, received some attention from the Irish parliament, Dáil Éireann, on a motion to note the Report of the Joint Committee on European Affairs on European Aspects of Drug Issues. In relation to cannabis, the Minister of State at the Department of Tourism, Sport and Recreation, with special responsibility for the Drug Problem, Mr Eoin Ryan, TD, referred to the sensitive issue of the decriminalisation of cannabis and noted that the Joint Committee's document did not come out with any specific recommendations. He noted, however, that it drew attention to the 'diversity of approaches in the European context' and recommended that 'an objective presentation of the facts relating to different strategies' must be part of any ongoing debate or policy formulation (Ryan, 2000). Thus, there is little evidence of a desire to decriminalise cannabis, as the findings of KAB1 (Bryan *et al.*, 2000), reported above, would also indicate.

The issue of heroin prescription was also referred to in Minister Ryan's speech. The Report of the Joint Committee on European Affairs referred to a 'heroin prescription' model, which was being piloted in Switzerland. The Minister observed, 'Obviously, such a radical approach has aroused much debate, and indeed controversy, not only in Europe but also here in Ireland. I note that while the European Affairs Committee recommends that the Irish health authorities should consider the need for and be authorised to develop what it describes as "innovative drug treatment measures", the Committee stops short of specifically recommending the introduction of the Swiss model here in Ireland' (Ryan, 2000). Recent statements from Government representatives have indicated that there are no plans to introduce heroin prescription projects in this country (Department of Health and Children, personal communication).

In the course of debates among professionals regarding the need for a variety of treatment options, the desirability / feasibility of the provision of injecting rooms is beginning to be discussed. The Merchant's Quay Project made a proposal in a submission to the National Drugs Strategy Review in this regard.

In conclusion, it would appear that as a result of political initiatives – including the devolution of more powers to local and regional levels, the growing involvement of the community and voluntary sectors in policy formulation and implementation, and the inter-agency and integrated approach to the drugs problem – a more open climate for debate on drug-related issues is developing.

5.6 References

Bryan, A., Moran, R., Farrell, E. & O'Brien, M. (2000). *Drug-Related Knowledge, Attitudes and Beliefs in Ireland: Report of a nation-wide survey.* Dublin: Drug Misuse Research Division, The Health Research Board.

Butler, S. (1997). The War on Drugs: Reports from the Irish front. *Economic and Social Review, 28*, 2, 157–175.

Comiskey, C. (1998). 'Estimating the Prevalence of Opiate Use in Dublin, Ireland during 1996'. Unpublished paper.

Corcoran, M. (1998). 'Making Fatima a Better Place to Live'. Report prepared for Fatima Groups United, Dublin. Unpublished.

Costello, L. & Howley, D. (2000). 'Working Towards Inclusion: A Feasibility Study on the Provision of Accommodation for People Sleeping Rough and Using Drugs in Dublin City'. Unpublished Report. Dublin: Dublin Simon Community and Merchant's Quay Project.

Coveney, E., Murphy-Lawless, J., Redmond, D. & Sheridan, S. (1999). *Prevalence, Profiles and Policy. A case study of drug use in north inner city Dublin.* Dublin: North Inner City Drug Task Force.

Cox, G. & Lawless, M. (1999). *Wherever I Lay My Hat. A study of out of home drug users.* Dublin: Merchant's Quay Project.

Dean, G., Bradshaw, J. & Lavelle, P. (1983). *Drug Misuse in Ireland, 1982 – 1983. Investigation in a north central Dublin area and in Galway, Sligo and Cork.* Dublin: The Medico-Social Research Board.

Dean, G., O'Hare, A., O'Connor, A., Melly, M. & Kelly, G. (1987). The 'opiate epidemic' in Dublin: Are we over the worst? *Irish Medical Journal, 80,* 5, 139–142.

DMRD (2000). 'Irish National Workshop on Prevalence Estimates as an Indicator of Drug Misuse'. Unpublished document, February 2000. Dublin: The Health Research Board.

Eastern Health Board (1997). *Review of Adequacy.* Dublin: Eastern Health Board.

EMCDDA (1997). *Estimating the Prevalence of Problem Drug Use in Europe.* EMCDDA Scientific Monograph Series No 1. Luxembourg: Office for Official Publications of the European Communities.

EMCDDA (1999) *Extended Annual Report on the State of the Drugs Problem in the European Union 1999.* Luxembourg: Office for Official Publications of the European Communities.

Fahey, T. (ed.) (1999). *Social Housing in Ireland: A study of success, failure and lessons learned.* Dublin: The Katherine Howard Foundation and Combat Poverty Agency.

Hogan, D. (1997). *The Social and Psychological Needs of Children of Drug Users: Report on exploratory study.* Dublin: The Children's Research Centre, Trinity College.

Howley, D. (2000). *An Analysis of the Dublin Simon Outreach Contacts for the Year ended December 1999.* Dublin: Simon Community.

Kelleher, T. (forthcoming). *Perceptions of Use, Availability, and the Responses to Illegal Drugs in Rural Ireland – A study of key informants.* Dublin: Drug Misuse Research Division, The Health Research Board.

Kelly, C. (1997). Eviction plans for drug pushers are flawed. *Poverty Today, 25* (April).

Loughran, H. (1996). Interview with Fergus McCabe. *Irish Social Worker, 14,* 3–4.

Loughran, H. (1999). Drugs policy in Ireland in the 1990s. In S. Quin, P. Kennedy, A. O'Donnell & G. Kiely (eds) *Contemporary Irish Social Policy.* Dublin: University College Dublin Press.

Mayock, P. (2000). *Choosers or Losers: Influences on young people's decisions about drugs in inner-city Dublin.* Dublin: The Children's Research Centre, Trinity College.

McAuliffe, R. & Fahey, T. (1999). Responses to Social Order Problems. In T. Fahey (ed.) *Social Housing in Ireland: A study of success, failure and lessons learned.* Dublin: The Katherine Howard Foundation and Combat Poverty Agency.

McCarthy, D. & McCarthy, P. (1995). *Dealing with the Nightmare: Drug use and intervention strategies in south inner-city Dublin.* Dublin: Community Response and Combat Poverty Agency.

McKeown, K., Fitzgerald, G. & Deegan, A. (1993). *The Merchant's Quay Project: A drugs/HIV service in the inner city of Dublin 1989 – 1992.* Dublin: The Merchant's Quay Project.

Memery, C. & Kerrins, L. (2000). *Estate Management and Anti-Social Behaviour in Dublin. A study of the impact of the Housing (Miscellaneous Provisions) Act 1997.* Dublin: Threshold.

Merchant's Quay Project (2000). *Annual Report 1999.* Dublin: The Merchant's Quay Project.

Ministerial Task Force (1996). *First Report of the Ministerial Task Force on Measures to Reduce the Demand for Drugs, 1996.* Dublin: Department of the Taoiseach.

Moran, R. (1977). 'Conceptualisation of Mental Illness and Attitudes Towards the Mentally Ill and Ex-Mental Patients'. Unpublished MSc thesis. Cork: Department of Psychology, University College Cork.

Moran, R. (1999). *The Availability, Use and Provision of Crèche Facilities in Association with Drug Treatment.* Dublin: The Health Research Board.

Moran, R., O'Brien, M. & Duff, P. (1997). *Treated Drug Misuse in Ireland. National report 1996.* Dublin: The Health Research Board.

Morley, C. (1998). *Consultation Process on the Future of St. Michael's Estate.* Dublin: St Michael's Estate Task Force.

Murphy, C. & Hogan, D. (1999). *Supporting Families through Partnership: Eastern Health Board (Area 5) Community Drugs Service.* Dublin: The Children's Research Centre, Trinity College.

O'Donnell, I. (1999). Criminal Justice Review, 1998. *Administration, 47,* 2, 175–211.

O'Gorman, A. (1998). Illicit drug use in Ireland: An overview of the problem and policy responses. *Journal of Drug Issues, 28,* 1, 155–166.

O'Gorman, A. (2000). *Eleven Acres, Ten Steps.* Dublin: Fatima Community Regeneration Team, Fatima Group United.

O'Hare, A. & O'Brien, M. (1992). *Treated Drug Misuse in the Greater Dublin Area: Report for 1990.* Dublin: The Health Research Board.

O'Higgins, K. (1996). *Treated Drug Misuse in the Greater Dublin Area: A review of five years 1990 – 1994.* Dublin: The Health Research Board.

O'Higgins, K. (1999). Social order problems. In T. Fahey (ed.) *Social Housing in Ireland: A study of success, failure and lessons learned.* Dublin: The Katherine Howard Foundation and Combat Poverty Agency.

O'Higgins, K. & O'Brien, M. (1995). *Treated Drug Misuse in the Greater Dublin Area: Report for 1994.* Dublin: The Health Research Board.

O'Kelly, R., Bury, G., Cullen, B. & Dean, G. (1988). The rise and fall of heroin use in an inner city area of Dublin. *Irish Medical Journal, 157,* (2), 35–38.

Ryan, E. (2000). Speech by the Minister of State, Mr Eoin Ryan, to Dáil Éireann on a motion to note the Report of the Joint Committee on European Affairs on European Aspects of Drug Issues, Thursday 18 May, 2000. Unpublished.

Silke, D. (1999). Housing policy. In S. Quin, P. Kennedy, A. O'Donnell & G. Kiely (eds) *Contemporary Irish Social Policy.* Dublin: University College Dublin Press.

Uhl, A. (2000). *Prevalence Estimate of Problematic Opiate Consumption in Austria.* Vienna: Ludwig Boltzmann Institute for Addiction Research (LBISucht).

Woods, M. (2000). Women, drug use and parenting. In Dublin: The views of professional workers in the drug treatment and social work fields. In A. Springer & A. Uhl (eds) *Illicit Drugs: Patterns of use – patterns of response,* Proceedings on the 10th Annual ESSD Conference on Drug Use and Drug Policy in Europe, September 1999. Innsbruch: Studienverlag.

CHAPTER 6

LAW ENFORCEMENT AND DRUG-RELATED CRIME

MARY O'BRIEN

6.1 Introduction

Drug-related data from law enforcement agencies are collected and published each year by An Garda Síochána. These data reflect the activities of the Gardaí and the Customs Service. Information includes charges for drug offences committed under the Misuse of Drugs Acts, 1977 and 1984, the quantity (by weight) and the number of seizures of illegal drugs, and the types of drugs involved.

Drug product purity is determined from seizures of drugs; analysis is carried out at the Forensic Science Laboratory of the Department of Justice, Equality and Law Reform. Information on the price of drugs is very scanty.

There is a dearth of research on drug-related crime in Ireland and it is an area that needs exploration. The National Advisory Committee on Drugs is planning to commission a study that will provide a preliminary overview of the issues involved in drug-related crime.

This chapter draws together available information on illicit drug offences recorded by law enforcement agencies, and on research done on drug-related crime in Ireland. Sections include:

6.2 Charges for Drug Offences

The use *per se* of drugs, excluding opium, is not a criminal offence in Ireland. Possession and trafficking/dealing/supplying are illegal activities under the Misuse of Drugs Acts, 1977 and 1984. In 1999 prosecutions under Section 3 of the Misuse of Drugs Acts, relating to possession offences, made up 68 per cent of the total prosecuted; 28 per cent were prosecuted under Section 15 of the Misuse of Drugs Acts, relating to drug-related trafficking offences (see Table 6.1). A breakdown by Garda regions[1] shows that most offences (38%) were in the Dublin metropolitan region (N=2,719), followed by 25 per cent in the Southern region (N=1,770). The proportion of possession offences was almost the same in these two areas: in Dublin, 29 per cent (N=1,437); in the Southern region, 29 per cent (N=1,394). Over half (56%, N=1,097) of the total trafficking (supply/dealing) offences were in Dublin.

With regard to the types of drugs involved, more than half (59%) of offences were cannabis-related and, of these, slightly more were in the Southern region than in Dublin (see Table 6.2). Ecstasy accounted for 14 per cent of drug-law offences and the majority of these were in the Southern region. The vast majority of heroin offences (852 out of a total of 887, 96%) were detected in the Dublin metropolitan region.

Trends over the five-year period from 1995 to 1999 show an increase in the number of drug charges, from 4,146 in 1995 to 7,137 in 1999 (see Table 6.3). There was a particularly sharp rise in cannabis offences in 1999: in 1998 cannabis offences (N=2,190) made up 39 per cent of total drug law offences, and in 1999 this increased to 59 per cent (N=4,185). Heroin offences have been steadily increasing over the five-year period. Amphetamine offences increased more than three-fold, from 138 in 1995 to 464 in 1999. The most dramatic jump in 1999 was in relation to ecstasy offences, which had been relatively stable in the preceding four years. This may have been as a result of a combination of an increased number of large-scale dance music events, and more intensive police activity both at such events and in general.

---

1   Since 1996 a regional command structure has been in place in An Garda Síochána and the country is divided into six separate regions - Eastern, Dublin Metropolitan, Northern, South-Eastern, Southern, and Western.

TABLE 6.1

Ireland 1999. Drug Law Offences by Type of Offence and Region. Numbers and Percentages.

Region	Possession (Section 3, MDA*)	Supply/Dealing (Section 15, MDA*)	Obstruction (Section 21, MDA*)	Other Offences	Total
Eastern	616	258	0	0	874 (12%)
Dublin Metropolis	1,437	1,097	127	58	2,719 (38%)
Northern	215	56	0	4	275 (4%)
South Eastern	534	103	11	4	652 (9%)
Southern	1,394	341	14	21	1,770 (25%)
Western	687	116	12	32	847 (12%)
Total	**4,883 (68%)**	**1,971 (28%)**	**164 (2%)**	**119 (2%)**	**7,137 (100%)**

Source: An Garda Síochána, *Annual Report of An Garda Síochána,* 1999.
* MDA = Misuse of Drugs Acts, 1977 & 1984.

TABLE 6.2

Ireland 1999. Drug Law Offences by Type of Drug and Region. Numbers and Percentages.

Region	Cannabis	Heroin	LSD	Ecstasy	Amphetamines	Cocaine	Other	Total
Eastern	543	19	3	200	83	9	17	874
Dublin Metropolis	1,208	852	2	211	70	126	250	2,719
Northern	187	0	1	60	16	4	7	275
South Eastern	437	1	11	81	92	6	24	652
Southern	1,227	12	5	368	108	10	40	1,770
Western	583	3	4	103	95	14	45	847
Total	**4,185 (59%)**	**887 (12%)**	**26 (0.003)%**	**1,023 (14%)**	**464 (7%)**	**169 (2%)**	**383 (5%)**	**7,137 (100%)**

Source: An Garda Síochána, *Annual Report of An Garda Síochána,* 1999.

TABLE 6.3

Ireland 1995–1999. Drug Law Offences by Type of Drug. Numbers.

Type of Drug	1995	1996	1997	1998	1999
Cannabis	2,600	1,834	2,671	2,190	4,185
Heroin	296	432	564	789	887
Other Opiates	0	0	6	0	0
Cocaine	30	42	97	88	169
Amphetamines	138	152	239	273	464
LSD	70	24	39	13	26
Ecstasy	645	340	475	439	1,023
Other Offences	385	454	65	1,839	383
Total	**4,146**	**3,278**	**4,156**	**5,631**	**7,137**

Source: An Garda Síochána, *Annual Reports of An Garda Síochána*, 1995 – 1999.

6.3 Trends in Quantities and Numbers of Drug Seizures

In Ireland it is not possible as yet to distinguish between Garda and Customs seizures in relation to the quantities and numbers of drugs seized. All seizures, by both agencies, are included in the annual reports of An Garda Síochána (An Garda Síochána, 1995, 1997, 1998, 1999a, 1999b). Garda and Customs authorities increasingly work on a collaborative basis and, following approaches by the Health Research Board (HRB) to both organisations, there is a willingness to provide separate information on seizures in the future.

Between 1995 and 1999 the number of seizures of all drugs, except for LSD, increased (see Table 6.4).

The number of seizures of all drugs has increased from 4,178 in 1995 to 7,318 in 1999. There are more seizures of cannabis than any other drug: the number increased from 3,205 in 1995 to 4,538 in 1999 (over the ten-year period 1990 to 1999, cannabis accounted for most of the drugs seized (see Figure 5.1 at Appendix 5)). Between 1995 and 1999, the number of heroin seizures more than tripled, from 209 to 767; cocaine increased five-fold, from 42 to 213; as did amphetamines, from 89 to 467. The number of ecstasy seizures increased quite considerably, from 571 in 1995 to 1,074 in 1999. It should be noted that 'ecstasy' can include various substances such as MDMA, MDEA, MDA, ephedrine or ketamine.

TABLE 6.4

Ireland 1995–1999. Seizures of Illicit Drugs. Numbers and Quantities.

Type of Drug	1995		1996		1997		1998		1999	
	N*	Q**	N*	Q**	N*	Q**	N*	Q**	N*	Q**
Cannabis	3,205	15,606.5	3,449	1,935.4	4,102	1,282.7	4,513	2,201.7	4,538	2,577.3
Heroin	209	6.4	664	10.8	599	8.2	884	38.3	767	17
Cocaine	42	21.8	93	642	157	11	151	333.2	213	85.6
Amphetamines	89	1.5	217	7.6	475	102.9	680	45	467	13.4
Ecstasy***	571	123,699	534	23,012	423	20,434	509	609,301	1,074	229,101
LSD	62	819	42	5,901	48	1,851	19	5,901	29	577
Benzodiazepines	0	0	152	7,146	219	4,942	181	2,885	175	15,393
Other Drugs	0	0	93	NA	159	NA	93	NA	55	NA
Total Number of Seizures	**4,178**		**5,244**		**6,182**		**7,030**		**7,318**	

Source: An Garda Síochána, Annual Reports of An Garda Síochána, 1995 – 1999.

* N = Number of seizures.

** Q = Quantity seized in kilograms; number of tablets in the case of ecstasy and benzodiazepines, and number of doses in the case of LSD.

***Ecstasy can include MDMA, MDEA, MDA, ephedrine or ketamine.

NA = Data not available.

The quantities of different types of drugs seized fluctuated from year to year. Apart from the very large seizure in 1995, the quantities of cannabis have been increasing each year. There was a very large seizure of illicit benzodiazepines (15,393 tablets/capsules) in 1999. The majority of these (13,389) were diazepam and one seizure alone that year comprised 7,800 diazepam. All benzodiazepines are controlled under Section 15 of the Misuse of Drugs Acts, 1977 and 1984: it is illegal to supply or deal in them other than by prescription. However, flunitrazepam (Rohypnol) and temazepam are controlled under both Section 15 and Section 3 of the Misuse of Drugs Acts: it is illegal to supply or possess them other than by prescription. Seized quantities of other drugs have tended to fluctuate over the same period, but in general quantities have been increasing since 1997 (see Figure 5.1 at Appendix 5).

6.4 Price and Purity of Drugs

It is not possible from the information available to distinguish between the price of drugs at street level and trafficking level. The Gardaí collect information on the street prices of drugs (see EMCDDA Standard Table 4.7 at Appendix 4). The data available up to now do not show much change in price over the past five years – heroin Ir£150/€190 per gram; cocaine Ir£80/€102 per gram; amphetamines Ir£9/€12 per gram. The price of an ecstasy tablet decreased from Ir£18/€22 in 1995 to Ir£9/€12 in 1999. However, this does not correspond with anecdotal evidence, which suggests that the prices fluctuate according to the market forces of supply and demand. For example, the price of heroin increases when supply is limited. No information is currently available on prices at trafficking level.

Drug seizures by the Gardaí are analysed at the Forensic Science Laboratory of the Department of Justice, Equality and Law Reform, to ascertain purity levels of heroin, cocaine and amphetamines. Cannabis potency is not analysed. Between 1995 and 1999 the purity levels of heroin decreased from 45 per cent to 33 per cent, and in 1999 a minimum purity level of 0.25 per cent was recorded. Purity levels of amphetamine seizures have also decreased somewhat, from 4.7 per cent in 1995 to 3 per cent in 1999. Cocaine purity levels are higher than in other drugs, but they have also fluctuated over the five-year period in a downward direction, from 47 per cent in 1995 to 41 per cent in 1999 (see Table 6.5).

TABLE 6.5
Ireland 1995–1999. Purity of Seized Drugs. Average Percentages.

Type of Seized Drug	1995	1996	1997	1998	1999
Heroin	45	49	46	35	33
Cocaine	47	62	54	38	41
Amphetamines	4.7	9.8	3.5	6	3

Source: Forensic Science Laboratory, Department of Justice, Equality and Law Reform, personal communication.

6.5 Availability of Different Drugs

Measuring the availability of drugs is a very difficult task, given the illicit nature of the activity. Special studies would need to be undertaken in order to explore the issues involved. In the Irish context there is, to date, very limited information available, and it has mostly been arrived at by indirect means.

The ESPAD 1995 nationwide school survey of 15- to 16-year-old post-primary school pupils (Hibell *et al.*, 1997) found that ecstasy was perceived as very easy to obtain in Ireland: 54 per cent said that obtaining it was 'very easy' or 'fairly easy'. Amphetamines were reported as being easy to obtain by one-third of the respondents.

Seizures may be taken as an indirect indication of the availability of illicit drugs. However, extreme caution must be used. The number of seizures and the amounts of illicit drugs seized can be affected by factors such as the resources committed to detection, changes in the quality of intelligence on illicit drugs trafficking, etc. In short, seizures cannot be used as a reliable indicator of trends in relation to the amount of drugs available on the market. The fact also, that not all drugs seized in Ireland are destined for the Irish market, but are in transit to elsewhere, further complicates the issue (GNDU, personal communication).

In Ireland there was a sizeable increase in the quantity of drugs seized in 1995 over previous years. This can be partly attributed to the setting up of the Garda National Drugs Unit (GNDU) in 1995 and to the activities of the Customs National Drugs Team. In that year there were two major seizures of cannabis, and one seizure of ecstasy contained 40,000 tablets.

6.6 Sources of Supply and Trafficking Patterns in Ireland

No research studies have been conducted in Ireland on drug supply sources or patterns of drug trafficking. The information in this section was obtained from personal contacts within the GNDU.

The sources of supply vary according to the type of drug. Cannabis comes mainly from Morocco, while some smaller seizures are known to have originated in Pakistan, Afghanistan and Lebanon (GNDU, personal communication). Some recent cannabis seizures are known to have originated in South Africa. Heroin seized in Ireland is thought to come from Asia, mainly Afghanistan, Pakistan, India and Laos. Cocaine is believed to originate in South America. The main place of origin for ecstasy seized in Ireland is the Netherlands, and to a lesser extent Belgium (GNDU, personal communication).

The Gardaí report that most of the trafficking in cannabis to Ireland takes place between Morocco and the south coast of Ireland. It is transported in articulated trucks using cross-channel ferries, and on sea-going yachts. The south-west coast is a major trans-shipment point. The bulk of heroin seizures are transported to Ireland through the United Kingdom, and some through the Netherlands. Individual drug couriers, travelling by air, bring smaller amounts from Europe.

The Gardaí believe that most of the drugs seized in Ireland in recent years have been for the home market. In the case of very large shipments it is speculated that Ireland, with its long coastline, sparsely populated in many areas, is used as an access point for transit to the United Kingdom and Europe. The Gardaí also believe that the distribution of drugs within Ireland is organised by networks of criminal gangs. In some cases these gangs involve members of the same family.

Sale patterns at street level in Dublin differ from location to location, with price and purity of drugs varying according to supply and demand factors.

6.7 Drug-Related Crime

The authors of the National Crime Forum Report (1998: 74) stated that they were 'deeply concerned with the impact of drug abuse on crime and the response of the criminal justice system to that issue'. The authors were impressed by suggestions to keep otherwise law-abiding young people out of the criminal justice system, for example, diverting young experimental users of cannabis and ecstasy into the Garda Juvenile Diversion Programme. The aim of this programme, established by An Garda Síochána, is to prevent crime and to provide an alternative for juvenile offenders. Rather than being dealt with under criminal law, young offenders enter the programme.

The case for the decriminalisation of certain drugs was presented to the Forum, which agreed that the issue was important and required more careful study. Those against decriminalisation argued that public opinion was opposed to such a change. A general population survey (Bryan, Moran, Farrell & O'Brien, 2000), the purpose of which was to examine drug-related knowledge, attitudes and beliefs in Ireland, supported this view: 76 per cent agreed that cannabis should be against the law. Results from the same study found that drug-related crime was considered to be a major problem in Ireland by 94 per cent (n=998) of those interviewed, and three-quarters of the sample felt that the drug problem was out of control.

A study to examine the association between drug use and crime in the Dublin metropolitan region was carried out by the Garda Research Unit (Keogh, 1997). The 'population' (N=4,105) was drawn from Garda records and Gardaí's local knowledge. It included all those who had come into contact with the Gardaí through being arrested, charged or suspected of criminal activity between August 1995 and September 1996. The inclusion criterion was 'individuals involved in hard drug use'; 'hard drugs' were defined as including opiates, stimulants, hypnotics and hallucinogens. During the study period 19,046 serious crimes were detected and 7,757 individuals were apprehended for these crimes: of these, 3,365 (43%) were identified as known hard-drug users. It was deduced that the hard-drug users were responsible for 12,583 (66%) of the crimes. A sub-sample (n=351) of these drug users agreed to be interviewed to provide more detailed information. It was found that 37 per cent had left school before the official school leaving age of 15, and 84 per cent were unemployed. While three-quarters of the respondents had at some time sought treatment for problem drug use and most had received it, a number (n=81) had never sought treatment of any kind. A majority said they had a poor understanding of the effects of drug use. It was found that 51 per cent had been involved in crime before their involvement with drugs; 48 per cent said family members were involved in crime.

In 1998 a study was conducted by the Garda Research Unit to explore the links between alcohol/drug use and crime (Millar, O'Dwyer & Finnegan, 1998). Gardaí at twenty-seven stations throughout the country (twelve in Dublin, fifteen in the other five Garda divisional regions) were asked for their 'informed opinion' (Millar et al., 1998: 2) as to whether alcohol or drugs were involved in offences where a person was 'arrested, charged, summonsed, or diverted under the Juvenile Diversion Programme' (Millar et al., 1998: 1). Offences under the Misuse of Drugs Acts and the Liquor Licensing Acts were excluded, presumably in an attempt to explore crimes associated with drug and alcohol users while excluding offences relating specifically to illicit drug and alcohol use. A total of 4,334 offences (no indication is given as to whether these refer to individuals or incidents) were noted during the study period (March to May 1998). Of these offences, 42 per cent were considered to be related to alcohol consumption; 17 per cent to drugs; and 4 per cent to alcohol and drugs (drugs were implicated in 913 cases). Alcohol was most likely to be associated with public order offences, while drugs were most often linked to robberies. In the drug-related offences, an opiate was the type of drug associated with offending behaviour in just over two-thirds of cases (see Table 6.6). There were regional differences: in Dublin an opiate was the drug most likely to be involved (83.1 % of cases), while outside Dublin cannabis (37.4 %) and ecstasy (25.9%) were the drugs most commonly cited (see Table 6.6).

TABLE 6.6
Ireland 1998. Garda Juvenile Diversion Programme. Drug-Related Crime.
Type of Drug by Area. Percentages and Numbers.

Main Drug Involved	Dublin	Other Areas	All Areas
Opiates	83.1%	20.1%	67.7%
Cannabis	13.5%	37.4%	19.4%
Ecstasy	0.9%	25.9%	7.1%
Amphetamines	0.9%	1.1%	1.0%
Barbiturates	0.6%	0.6%	0.6%
Cocaine	0.2%	1.1%	0.4%
Hallucinogens	0.2%	0.0%	0.1%
Other	0.6%	13.8%	3.8%
Total %	100.0%	100.0%	100.0%
Valid n	534	174	708
Missing n	136	69	205
Total n	670	243	913

Source: Millar *et al.*, 1998.

6.8 Summary

Trends over the five-year period from 1995 to 1999 show an increase in the number of drug charges, from 4,146 in 1995 to 7,137 in 1999. Most prosecutions for drug offences were for possession of controlled substances and the drug most commonly involved was cannabis. In 1999 more cannabis offences were detected in the Southern region (N=1,227) than in Dublin (N=1,208). The majority of heroin offences (852 out of a total of 887) were in Dublin.

There was an increase in the number of seizures of drugs, from 4,178 in 1995 to 7,318 in 1999. Cannabis accounted for most of the drugs seized; the number of cannabis seizures increased from 3,205 in 1995 to 4,538 in 1999. During the same period the number of heroin seizures more than tripled, from 209 to 767.

According to the information available, the price of drugs has not changed much in five years except in the case of ecstasy tablets. The price decreased from Ir£18/€22 per tablet in 1995 to Ir£9/€12 per tablet in 1999.

Purity levels of drugs have fallen over the five-year period 1995 to 1999, particularly so in the case of heroin – from 45 per cent pure in 1995 to 33 per cent pure in 1999.

Special studies are needed to determine the availability of different drugs, in order to better inform prevention strategies. No research studies have been conducted in Ireland on drug supply sources or patterns of drug trafficking; neither is there any research available on the price of drugs

A Garda study to examine the association between drug use and crime in the Dublin metropolitan region found that hard-drug users were responsible for 66 per cent of the crime committed over a period of a year, between August 1995 and September 1996. Of a sub-sample of 351 respondents, three-quarters had at some time sought treatment for problem drug use and most had received it; however, a number (n=81) had never sought treatment of any kind. A majority said they had a poor understanding of the effects of drug use. Fifty-one per cent said that they had been involved in crime before their involvement with drugs; 48 per cent said family members were involved in crime.

6.9 References

Bryan, A., Moran, R., Farrell, E. & O'Brien, M. (2000). *Drug-Related Knowledge, Attitudes and Beliefs in Ireland. Report of a nation-wide survey.* Dublin: The Health Research Board.

An Garda Síochána (1995). *Annual Report of An Garda Síochána 1995.* Dublin: The Stationery Office.

An Garda Síochána (1997). *Annual Report of An Garda Síochána 1996.* Dublin: The Stationery Office.

An Garda Síochána (1998). *Annual Report of An Garda Síochána 1997.* Dublin: The Stationery Office.

An Garda Síochána (1999a). *Annual Report of An Garda Síochána 1998.* Dublin: The Stationery Office.

An Garda Síochána (1999b). *Annual Report of An Garda Síochána 1999.* Dublin: The Stationery Office.

Hibell, B., Andersson, B., Bjarnason, T., Kokkevi, A., Morgan, M. & Narusk, A. (1997). *The 1995 ESPAD Report. Alcohol and other drug use among students in 26 European countries*. Stockholm and Strasbourg: The Swedish Council for Alcohol and other Drugs (CAN), Stockholm, and Council of Europe, Pompidou Group, Strasbourg.

Keogh, E. (1997). *Illicit Drug Use & Related Criminal Activity in the Dublin Metropolitan Area*. Dublin: An Garda Síochána.

Millar, D., O'Dwyer, K. & Finnegan, M. (1998*). Alcohol and Drugs as Factors in Offending Behaviour: Garda survey*. Research Report No 7/98. Tipperary: Garda Research Unit.

National Crime Forum (1998). *Report of the National Crime Forum 1998*. Dublin: Institute of Public Administration.

CHAPTER 7

DEMAND REDUCTION INTERVENTIONS

EIMEAR FARRELL, ROSALYN MORAN AND LUCY DILLON

7.1 Introduction

Demand reduction embraces a wide range of activities aimed at decreasing the demand for drugs at an individual or collective level. Thus, it includes interventions in the areas of prevention, harm minimisation and treatment. This chapter begins by providing a definition of demand reduction and setting the national policy context. It then describes a number of demand reduction interventions under the following headings:

7.3 Primary Prevention
7.4 Reduction of Drug-Related Harm
7.5 Treatment
7.6 After-Care and Re-Integration
7.7 Interventions in the Criminal Justice System
7.8 Specific Targets and Settings

The list of interventions is not exhaustive, but rather reflects those projects known to the Drug Misuse Research Division (DMRD) of the Health Research Board (HRB). The DMRD adopted a number of strategies to identify relevant interventions – written requests to a range of personnel (e.g. regional drugs co-ordinators) active in the area of demand reduction in each of the regional health board areas; advertisements in DrugNet Ireland; and work undertaken as part of the EDDRA project (see Section 7.3.6).

The chapter concludes with an overview of the issues of quality assurance, training and the dissemination of information as they relate to the whole field of demand reduction.

The interventions are described in accordance with the format provided by the European Monitoring Centre for Drugs and Drug Addiction (EMCDDA) (see General Introduction).

7.2 Definition and National Context

The EMCDDA has provided an operational definition of demand reduction:

> [Demand reduction] comprises interventions which are aimed at decreasing the demand for drugs at an individual or at a collective level. Interventions aimed at reducing the harmful consequences of drug use are also included. The scope of demand reduction intervention is wide and consists of many facets. At one end of the continuum, preventive action aims at not letting a demand for drugs arise at all, having a wide range of diverse actions targeted at large groups, e.g. school programmes, mass media programmes and community based programmes. At the other end are measures of a limited scope directed at individual drug users, e.g. outreach work, treatment, prevention of HIV infection and AIDS. Generally each action leading to a drug user refraining from drug use at a certain point in time, or refraining from especially harmful practices involved in drug use is comprised by the operational concept of demand reduction. (EMCDDA, 1996)

This chapter focuses on demand reduction projects in the area of prevention, harm minimisation and treatment.

The main government departments involved in demand reduction in Ireland are the Department of Health and Children, the Department of Tourism, Sport and Recreation and the Department of Education and Science. At an operational level, the regional health boards and the community and voluntary sectors play a vital role in the delivery of demand reduction activities. The new local government structures defined under the National Development Plan 2000 - 2006 (NDP, 2000) also have a role (see Chapter 1).

The Department of Health and Children, through the regional health boards, plays an active role in drug treatment. Through its Health Promotion Unit, the Department is responsible for the dissemination of information on drug misuse to the general public and to at-risk groups. In 1999 and 2000 each health board was provided with additional funding to continue to develop all aspects of their drug prevention and treatment services. The Department also provides funding to all health boards to collect information on drug prevention in their areas.

The Department of Tourism, Sport and Recreation funds demand reduction activities through the Local Drug Task Forces (LDTFs), which were established to provide a strategic local response by statutory, community and voluntary sectors, to the drugs problem in areas where drug misuse is a serious problem. The LDTFs comprise representatives from statutory bodies such as the health boards, Gardaí, local authorities, FÁS and the vocational education committees (VECs), as well as from voluntary and community groups. The Department also funds initiatives under the Young People's Facilities and Services Fund (YPFSF) (see Section 7.3.3; Chapter 1; and Moran, Dillon, O'Brien, Mayock & Farrell, forthcoming).

The Department of Education and Science operates mainly through the formal education system. The departments of Health and Education liaise closely on a bilateral basis and are involved in intersectoral structures set up to address the drugs issue (see Chapter 1). Both departments also support initiatives in the non-formal education sector, as does the Department of Tourism, Sport and Recreation.

The Department of Justice, Equality and Law Reform and the Department of Social, Community and Family Affairs also fund initiatives in the area of demand reduction.

The National Health Promotion Strategy (Department of Health and Children, 2000a) outlines a number of objectives relating to drug misuse. The principal aim of the strategy is to support best-practice models for the promotion of the non-use of drugs and the minimisation of the harm caused by drugs. The objectives are to :

- ensure each health board has in place a comprehensive drugs education and prevention strategy;
- continue to support the implementation of existing drug-related health promotion programmes;
- work in partnership with relevant government departments (e.g. Department of Education and Science) and other bodies to co-ordinate health promotion activities; and
- develop prevention and education programmes, with particular emphasis on schools and the youth sector and on interventions in areas where drug misuse is most prevalent.

There has been a substantial increase in the number of projects and programmes developed in the demand reduction area in recent years. This is largely due to increased efforts to address the issue of social exclusion and drug misuse, particularly in areas where a serious drug problem exists. Considerable government funding has been made available in this context (see Chapter 1, and Moran *et al.*, forthcoming).

7.3 Primary Prevention

This section describes primary prevention projects in the following areas:

7.3.1 Infancy and Family
7.3.2 School Programmes
7.3.3 Youth Programmes outside Schools
7.3.4 Community Programmes
7.3.5 Telephone Helplines
7.3.6 Mass Media Campaigns and Internet-Based Projects

7.3.1 Infancy and Family

The **Lorien Project**, based in Tallaght (a large suburb of Dublin), provides a range of early-years services to the children and siblings of drug users. It also provides support services for the families of drug users. The project, managed by Barnardos (a large, voluntary childcare charity), has three staff members and provides a service for sixty families.

The **Eastern Regional Health Authority (ERHA)** is in the process of employing three drug-liaison midwives to make contact with substance-misusing pregnant women and to liaise between the obstetric hospitals and the drug-treatment services. The midwives are responsible for ensuring that the medical, psychological, obstetrical and social needs of each woman have been accurately assessed and for preparing a detailed clinical/psychological/social care plan for each woman (Eastern Health Board, 1998).

The government has made available IR£2.4 million/€3.05 million for each year between 1998 and 2000 to set up **family-support projects** for children and families at risk within particular communities.

Projects have been established in a number of locations, both urban and rural, throughout the country, including Dublin, Cork, Galway and Sligo (Department of Health and Children, 2000a). The projects described here include:

- The Springboard Initiative throughout Ireland;
- Fás le Chéile in the North Western Health Board area;
- Family Communication and Self Esteem in Cork and Kerry; and
- Kilkenny Drugs Initiative Family Support Group.

The **Springboard Initiative** was established by the Department of Health and Children to assist vulnerable children and their families in thirteen areas throughout the country. Projects established under the initiative work intensively with children and their families and provide necessary supports, in a co-ordinated manner, to strengthen the coping capacity of families.

Fás le Chéile (Grow Together) is a support programme for parents of primary-school children, set up by the North Western Health Board (NWHB), to train parents to act as group leaders and to run courses for parents in conjunction with local primary schools. The programme is aimed at mothers and fathers who have children in primary schools and who are interested in meeting other parents for support and information in relation to the healthy development of their family. It is based on social learning theory and emphasises group discussion and peer-led facilitation. The overall purpose of the programme is to promote a positive relationship between parents and their children. The substance misuse component of the programme encourages dialogue among family members about drugs, provides accurate information about drugs and alcohol, increases awareness of the importance of self-esteem in preventing substance abuse and builds parents' confidence and skills in handling difficult situations. An evaluation (Gallagher, 1999) revealed that the parents were very satisfied with the programme. Participants reported that their communications and listening skills had improved with both their partners and their children. Participants also experienced an increased confidence in their own parenting skills and they felt that the social learning approach was conducive to learning. A further evaluation of the programme is planned for 2001.

Family Communication and Self Esteem[1] was developed, initially in Cork and Kerry, in response to a need for parents to develop skills that would help them contribute to the prevention of misuse of alcohol, drugs and other substances. The programme focuses on parents as the primary educators and seeks to exploit the connection between prevention of drug misuse and family communication. The programme has two main components – parenting education and drug education. The programme emphasises empowering and enabling participants to help themselves, building up self-esteem and developing interpersonal skills and resources. An evaluation of the programme indicated

1   See EDDRA database for further information on this project, http://www. reitox.emcdda. org:8008/eddra/. It may also be viewed through the HRB website, www.hrb.ie

that both parents and tutors responded very positively to the programme (Ruddle, 1993). Parents highlighted many learning outcomes and provided examples of how they had been putting their new skills into practice.

Kilkenny Drugs Initiative (KDI) Family Support Group, based in Kilkenny city, was set up for parents and partners of substance misusers in Kilkenny city and county. The group meets once a week for two hours and offers an opportunity for people to come together to share information and talk about their experiences. It also offers the opportunity for personal healing through aromatherapy, meditation, and the chance to engage in substance misuse education programmes.

7.3.2 School Programmes

The Department of Education and Science, in collaboration with the Department of Health and Children, has developed specific substance-abuse prevention programmes for both primary and secondary school children. The programmes, known respectively as **On My Own Two Feet**[2] and **Walk Tall**, emphasise self-esteem, feelings, influences, drug awareness and decision-making skills to help children withstand pressures to use drugs.

An outcome evaluation of 'On My Own Two Feet' found that, compared to a control group, students who participated in the programme had less positive attitudes to drug/alcohol use, and stronger beliefs in the negative outcomes of such use (Morgan, Morrow, Sheehan & Lillis, 1996). A formative evaluation by Morgan (1998) found that the 'Walk Tall' programme incorporated the approaches demonstrated to be most effective in preventing substance abuse. The evaluation also indicated that there was a very high rate of satisfaction with the programme among teachers who participated in it.

It is planned that the new Social, Personal and Health Education (S.P.H.E.) programme, to be introduced in second-level schools from September 2000, will subsume 'On My Own Two Feet', and that S.P.H.E. will become an integral part of the curriculum for all junior-cycle students. A national co-ordinator has been appointed to implement the S.P.H.E. programme and ten regional development officers are being recruited. The initiative is being supported by the departments of Education and Science and of Health and Children and the regional health boards. The regional development officers being recruited will work in partnership with Health Promotion personnel from the health boards. They will also collaborate with other statutory and voluntary bodies to offer a co-ordinated support service.

---

2 See footnote 1.

At the regional level, a school-based programme known as the **Healthy Schools Project** has been introduced. This initiative was developed by the North Eastern Health Board (NEHB) for schools in the NEHB catchment area. The central objective of the programme is to encourage students to take responsibility for their own health and behaviour. The programme emphasises the development of life skills, including decision making, assertiveness and self-esteem. An evaluation of the programme indicated that there were significant differences between the pilot and the control group on items relating to acceptance of responsibility, self-esteem, positive outcomes in adulthood and attitudes to substance abuse (Morgan, 1997a).

A locally-based project, situated in one of the major urban areas in the Dublin region, the **Killinarden Drug Primary Prevention Group**, runs a number of drug education/self-esteem programmes in schools in Killinarden. The project is run by local parents and the programmes are delivered to children at both primary and secondary level. This project has two part-time staff and occasional facilitators.

7.3.3 Youth Programmes outside Schools

The **Young People's Facilities and Services Fund (YPFSF)** was established by the Government in 1998. Its objective is to assist in the development of preventative strategies in a targeted manner, through the development of youth facilities, including sport and recreation facilities and services, in disadvantaged areas, where a significant drugs problem exists or has the potential to develop. The aim of the fund is to attract 'at-risk' young people in disadvantaged areas into these facilities and activities, thereby diverting them from becoming involved in substance misuse. Several projects are funded through this programme.

The **Copping On Programme** is a national crime awareness programme, targeted at early school leavers and young people at risk. It was established in 1996. The programme aims to reduce the risk and incidence of offending behaviour among young people and to decrease harmful and damaging behaviour, such as bullying, alcohol and drug use. There are two main components in the programme. The first component provides training for professionals who work with early school leavers and with young people at risk. The training focuses on creating a greater awareness of the factors influencing offending behaviour, examination of personal values and underlying principles, and identifying effective responses for the target group. The second component provides training for early school leavers and young people at risk. The course focuses on similar topics to the training for professionals, including communications, relationships, drugs and alcohol, moral education and understanding the criminal justice system. At the end of the programme, individuals are invited to give feedback through specially-designed evaluations. A recent evaluation (Bowden, 1998) concluded that both trainers and young participants reacted positively to the programme.

The **National Youth Health Programme** is a partnership between the National Youth Council of Ireland, the Health Promotion Unit of the Department of Health and Children and the Youth Affairs Section of the Department of Education and Science. The aim of the programme is to provide broad-based, flexible youth-health education in the non-formal education sector. It assists youth workers, leaders and volunteers working in the youth services and other community groups in addressing the health needs of young people. The service provides training at organisational, regional and national levels, and gives advice and support to youth and community organisations that are developing their own health education programmes and initiatives.

The project has developed a Youth Work Support Pack, which deals with the drugs issue. The pack is divided into four sections: (1) youth work in a drug-using society; (2) youth work responses to drug use; (3) policy development; and (4) supporting information.

Sound Decisions,[3] established in the NEHB area, is targeted at nightclub and disco staff and young people attending discos and nightclubs. One of the main objectives of the project is to raise awareness of the dangers of drugs among young people and nightclub staff. It is also designed to increase the competence of nightclub staff in dealing with drug-related issues. The programme consists of training sessions to inform nightclub staff about the legal implications relating to drug use, to enable them to recognise signs of drug use and to respond effectively to drug-related emergencies. Promotional materials, such as pins, posters, leaflets, stickers and t-shirts, are used to highlight for club-goers the dangers associated with drugs.

The **Staying Alive Campaign**, a Dublin Safer Dance Initiative, was initiated and funded by the Dun Laoghaire / Rathdown Local Drug Task Force and was subsequently funded by the Eastern Health Board (EHB). The programme is designed to provide training and support to nightclub staff in order to allow them to respond more effectively to drug-related situations in nightclubs (Harding, 2000). The first and second phases of this project involve the organisation of training programmes for club owners/managers and door supervisors, and focus on increasing participants' knowledge about drugs, exploring their attitudes towards drugs, and examining legal, health and safety issues. The third phase of the project is designed to allow young club-goers to obtain access to accurate information

---

3   See footnote 1.

about drugs. This phase, currently in the pilot stage, will involve distributing information about drugs in the form of a small credit-card-sized booklet, known as the Vital Information Pack (VIP), through a number of venues, including third-level colleges and clubs (Harding, 2000). Phases four and five of the project have also been planned. In phase four, a one-day conference will be organised to gain support from the music/dance industry for the development of acceptable policies in dance venues across the ERHA region. Phase five will involve standardising training for door supervisors and providing the different training elements in modular form. No statistics on programme participation are available.

Funding has been approved for the establishment of the **Health Advice Café** in Galway's city centre. Galway is located in the Western Health Board (WHB) area. The purpose of the café will be to offer young people direct access to health services and to health information and advice. The café will incorporate a range of drug prevention and education strategies and provide information about available treatment services. It will also emphasise 'fun drug-free activities', to show young people that it is possible to have a good time without using drugs.

7.3.4 Community Programmes

There has been a proliferation of local community-based drug initiatives, particularly in relation to drug awareness, over the last few years. This is due to the increased availability of funding for projects to tackle the drugs problem. The initiatives organised by community groups include drug awareness programmes, family support groups, and the development of strategies to reduce the demand for drugs in local areas. A few examples of the different types of initiatives are presented here. The final three projects described (JADD, Cabra Resource Centre and the Crinan Project) have been evaluated under the LDTF evaluation initiative.

The **County Waterford Community-Based Drugs Initiative (CWCBDI)** was established in November 1999 and aims to:

* increase awareness of drug-related issues;
* develop strategies for the reduction of demand for drugs;
* support local communities in responding to local needs relating to drug-related issues; and
* improve the quality of life of those affected by drug misuse.

The project is currently involved in the following initiatives – determining what local people think about drug-related issues (needs analysis); providing drug awareness programmes to youth groups and schools; running parent support groups; and promoting the development of drug policies in various organisations.

CWCBDI has adopted a multi-faceted approach to its work. Statutory, community and voluntary organisations are represented on the management committee of the project. This means that local people are involved in the management of the project and in making any major decisions relating to the project. It also ensures that the work is consultative and inclusive of local needs and issues.

Drug Questions – Local Answers is a community-based training programme produced by the Health Promotion Unit of the Department of Health and Children. It is aimed at health/education professionals, Gardaí, community groups, doctors, youth workers etc. The objective of the five-unit, ten-hour training course is to help participants cope better with alcohol- and drug-related problems that they meet in their work/lives, and to contribute to community-based responses to the drugs problem. The Health Promotion Unit of the Department of Health and Children, in conjunction with the eight regional health boards, has provided convenor-training programmes to show instructors how to use the training materials effectively.

The **Crew Network**, based in the ERHA area, is a non-profit organisation dedicated to the care, rehabilitation, education and occupational re-integration of those affected by substance misuse. The network is engaged in a number of demand-reduction activities, including school-based programmes and parent and community awareness nights. It has developed a community leadership and substance-misuse awareness course, accredited by National University of Ireland (NUI), Maynooth. The Crew Network also provides a family and counselling service.

The **Drug Awareness Programme (DAP)**, operated by a registered charity, Crosscare, helps groups and communities in the Dublin area to develop a comprehensive approach to drug prevention. DAP provides a wide range of services, including needs assessment for local drug prevention, drug awareness training and peer education programmes. DAP also provides a counselling, support and telephone helpline service.

Community Addiction Response Programme (CARP) began as a partnership between the local community and a medical practitioner in the west Dublin area of Tallaght. The aim was to provide a methadone prescription service. The service has since expanded to include various activities for those receiving methadone, including artwork, homeopathy, bowling and football. The overall purpose of the programme is to deliver a user-friendly, client-centred service to opiate users in Killinarden, so that they can re-integrate themselves into the community. The programme is targeted at those aged sixteen and older who are problem drug users, but it will also cater for younger drug addicts who present for treatment. While the programme is primarily targeted at those with heroin addiction, it also offers a service for those abusing other substances. CARP also aims to help families affected by drug use and has established a support group for parents of drug users.

CARP has forged links with various vocational training programmes in the area, to allow clients in receipt of methadone maintenance to gain access to further training. CARP also produces a newsletter, which is distributed to the local community every quarter, and members of the organisation give talks on drugs to local schools. An evaluation report (Bowden, 1997) showed that participants generally viewed the programme in positive terms and the programme allowed participants to develop the ability to resist heroin.

Ballymun Youth Action Project offers a range of services to individuals and families in the Ballymun area of Dublin. There are three main components to the project: (1) individual and family services; (2) education and training; and (3) community work. Advice, referral, information, counselling and family support are offered under the individual and family services component. The education and training component provides community education on drug abuse, develops drug/alcohol awareness programmes tailored to the needs of specific groups and delivers primary-school educational programmes. The community work component consists of liaising and networking with other groups and agencies, contributing to policy development, empowering local people to participate in responding at a local level, and researching how community development principles can be put into practice in relation to drug issues.

Ballymun Community Action Programme acts as a community resource centre and development programme and is run by a management committee of local people who live and work in Ballymun. It aims to respond to the needs of local groups, initiate activity where gaps in service provision may exist, and draw lessons from the experiences of local groups that can inform policy. The project is actively involved in influencing policy from a community perspective and in encouraging local people to contribute positively to policy development in relation to the drugs issue.

The **Adult Substance Misuse Education Programme**, developed by the Kilkenny Drugs Initiative (KDI), is designed to help build the capacity of local communities to deal with the issue of substance abuse in their local area, by enabling participants to facilitate and train other people in the community. The programme is delivered to groups of between six and twelve people, and consists of between two and five sessions, each lasting two hours. The programme covers aspects of substance misuse such as the effects of drugs, signs and symptoms of drug use and drugs in a legal context.

Jobstown Assisting Drug Dependency (JADD) was established in 1996, by a group of local people, in response to the growing problem of heroin abuse in Jobstown, a suburb of Dublin City. JADD emerged from a series of local community meetings concerning the drugs problem. The purpose of the programme is to support and help drug users and their families to re-integrate into the community. The project works with active drug misusers, drug misusers who are drug free, and drug misusers who are participating in methadone programmes. The majority of JADD clients are male, early school-leavers and unemployed. Clients hear about JADD through word of mouth, contact with healthcare professionals or meeting current clients.

One of the main services offered by JADD is methadone maintenance and gradual detoxification. JADD also provides a counselling service, a drop-in centre, primary health care and after care. The drop-in facility is open five days a week. The counselling and drop-in services are also available to family members. Clients can take part in education and training programmes such as drama, art, computer skills, literacy skills, creative writing, career guidance, job searching and sport/fitness. JADD has a Family Support Group, which meets once a week for two hours. JADD also aims to inform and educate the local community regarding drug addiction and drug-related diseases and to network with other local community groups. A recent evaluation (O'Rourke, 2000) found that participants generally viewed the programme in positive terms, and that JADD had made a significant contribution to the quality of life and provision of opportunities for many people living in the Jobstown area.

Cabra Resource Centre, established in September 1999, was set up as a 'drop-in' centre for individuals and families in the community who were concerned about alcohol and substance abuse. The centre provides brief intervention counselling and an information service and is equipped with a multi-media library. It also acts as a referral agency and organises family support groups. An evaluation in 2000 (Burtenshaw & O'Reilly, 2000) concluded that the project was delivering what it set out to deliver. Strengths and weaknesses, and facilitating and constraining factors relating to the project, were identified.

The **Crinan Project,** based in Dublin and funded by the City of Dublin Youth Services Board, was established to cater for young drug users (fifteen to eighteen years of age), who are especially vulnerable and have few service or treatment opportunities. Participants have usually left school at a very young age and have had frequent involvement in illegal activities. The project is holistic and emphasises not only medical intervention but also the provision of enabling skills and drug-free alternatives. The project has two main components – a day programme and an after-hours/evening component. The main services offered by the day programme include:

- individual and group therapy;
- medical services including detoxification and drug testing;
- youthwork; and
- family support.

The after-hours component, designed to complement the day programme, includes evening activities, weekend events, literacy and education support, and youth work training and networking. An evaluation (Morgan, 1997b & 2000) concluded that the approach taken in the programme was in line with the most effective approaches to treatment.

7.3.5 Telephone Helplines

EHB Helpline, a free telephone helpline, was established by the Eastern Health Board (EHB) during 1997 and is available five days a week from 10 am to 5 pm. It was set up to provide a confidential service, offering information, support, guidance and referral for those concerned with any aspect of drug misuse.

Waterford Drug Helpline provides a telephone counselling and information service between 10 am and 12 noon Monday to Friday, and on two evenings a week from 8 pm to 10 pm. The helpline has ten unpaid volunteers. The service was set up to educate the general public, particularly parents and young people, about drug-related issues and to provide a listening service to those affected by drug use. The service aims to be easy to contact, confidential and non-judgemental. It also provides factual information about drugs and their effects and gives out details of drug-related services in the Waterford region. In 1999 a total of 1,270 calls were received. The majority of these calls related to cannabis/ alcohol (31.3%), ecstasy (30.9%) and amphetamines (24.2%) (Waterford Helpline, personal communication, 1999). The Helpline is a member of the European Foundation of Drug Helplines (PESAT).

Cork Helpline, provided by the Southern Health Board (SHB), offers information on prevention and service provision. It is a charge-free service and operates on weekdays from 1 pm to 2 pm.

7.3.6 Mass Media Campaigns and Internet-Based Projects

The Health Promotion Unit of the Department of Health and Children disseminates information on drugs and their effects on an on-going basis. Increasingly, the possibilities afforded by Information and Communications Technologies (ICT) are beginning to be explored in the demand-reduction area.[4] Foremost among such projects is the European Database on Demand Reduction Activities (EDDRA).

EDDRA is a database that describes state-of-the-art drug demand-reduction activities in the fifteen member states of the European Union (EU). It was developed by the EMCDDA to collect objective, reliable and comparable information on demand-reduction activities across Europe. EDDRA is designed to meet the needs of practitioners, researchers, and policy makers involved in the planning and implementation of demand-reduction activities. Projects on prevention, treatment and rehabilitation and criminal justice initiatives in Ireland and Europe are included. It is a good, easily accessible source of ideas for new projects.[5]

Underlying the development of EDDRA was a commitment to project quality and evaluation. Projects in the EDDRA database are chosen to represent 'best practice' in demand reduction. To be eligible for inclusion in EDDRA, a project must have been evaluated. A number of Irish projects are included in EDDRA and these will be added to on an ongoing basis.[6]

HYPER, a bi-monthly magazine, was launched in Spring 1999 by the project promoter, Soilse, which is a rehabilitation programme now in the ERHA. *HYPER,* which is an acronym for Health, Youth, Promotion, Education and Rehabilitation, acts as a voice for young people affected by drugs. It is funded through the EHB, by Youthstart and an EU Employment Initiative for eighteen- to twenty-year-olds. It is produced by six former drug users, as part of a rehabilitation project, and aims to bring young people a magazine to which they can relate and which critically addresses their lifestyles 'without preaching or scare-mongering'. The magazine includes interviews, book and theatre reviews, and cartoons and articles that challenge peoples' attitudes towards drugs, young people and health. In July 1999 *HYPER* won an award in the British-based Total Publishing Awards competition for design innovation. The magazine was selected from over 400 entries.

7.4 Reduction of Drug-Related Harm

7.4.1 Outreach Work

Each regional health board is developing its outreach capacity as part of overall service development in the drugs area. Outreach workers provide needle exchange, support for sex

---

4   For example, the DMRD participates in the EU PrevNet project – www.prevnet.net
5   The database is located on the website of the EMCDDA at: www.reitox.emcdda.org:8008/ eddra/. It may also be viewed through the HRB website: www.hrb.ie
6   Readers with evaluated projects, which they would like to enter into EDDRA, should contact Martin Keane, EDDRA Manager for Ireland, at the DMRD of the HRB.

workers, and referrals for methadone maintenance. According to the EMCDDA Insights report, outreach workers in Ireland emphasise the importance of a community presence, which enables them to 'intervene and fast-track individuals to treatment while concentrating on making contact and increasing service accessibility' (EMCDDA, 1999: 131).

ERHA Outreach programme targets injecting drug users (IDUs), women in prostitution and gay or bisexual men (EMCDDA, 1999). It aims to:

- reach IDUs who are not in touch with services and provide them with information on HIV and its prevention;
- encourage and facilitate referrals to drug-treatment agencies; and
- provide information to community groups about HIV.

7.4.2 Low-Threshold Services

A **Mobile Clinic** was established in the EHB area in 1996. The service is low threshold and provides initial services to the more chaotic drug user, who is addicted to an opiate, is injecting and is incapable of stabilisation on methadone maintenance. Low-threshold services place more emphasis on harm reduction than on abstinence. A second mobile clinic was introduced in 2000, increasing the number of areas where drug users can avail of this service. No evaluation results are available. No information on specific training is available. The DMRD is currently carrying out a research study to assess the needs of users of this service and their experiences of this and other drug-treatment services.

7.4.3 Prevention of Infectious Diseases

Drug users who present for treatment at any of the statutory drug-treatment services are routinely offered HIV and hepatitis C testing. Needle exchanges are operated only in the ERHA, which covers the greater Dublin area, where the vast majority of IDUs reside.

According to the report of the National AIDS Strategy Committee, recent HIV statistics indicate that interventions with IDUs are effective in reducing transmission rates among this 'at-risk' group (Department of Health and Children, 2000b). However, there was an increase in the number of drug users who tested positive for HIV in 1999. In 1999, sixty-nine drug users tested positive for HIV, compared to twenty-six and twenty-one for 1998 and 1997 respectively (Department of Health and Children, 2000b).

A nationwide antenatal/HIV-testing programme has been established, with the aim of reducing perinatal transmission, through the antenatal treatment of HIV-positive women with anti-retroviral drugs and careful management at delivery (Department of Health and Children, 2000b). No evaluation results are available. Training for midwives and others involved in the programme was provided in all health board areas by a team including expert clinicians, a midwife and a social worker.

The **Health Promotion Unit, Merchant's Quay Project,** operates the largest needle exchange in the country. It is aimed at drug users who inject heroin, and offers a drop-in service, which is open Monday to Friday, from 2 pm to 4.30 pm. The Health Promotion Unit offers a range of services to its clients: it provides needles and syringes, sterile water, filters, swabs, citric acid and condoms; it acts as a source of referral to other drug-treatment services; and it offers a nursing service. This nursing service provides clients with basic wound care, and deals with other health issues such as scabies, athlete's foot and any other conditions with which clients present. When appropriate, referrals are made to other services and clients may also apply for a medical card. Encouraging clients to engage in specialist contact, such as having an HIV test or receiving the hepatitis B vaccination, is also considered an integral part of the Health Promotion Unit's work. A recent evaluation (Cox & Lawless, 2000) found that the Health Promotion Unit had a positive impact on clients' drug-using behaviour. There was a reduction in the frequency of injecting and the incidence of sharing and an increase in condom use reported by clients at the three-month follow-up visit.

7.5 Treatment

7.5.1 Treatment and Health Care at National Level

The Government Strategy to Prevent Drug Misuse (National Co-ordinating Committee on Drug Misuse, 1991) recognised that the treatment, care and management of drug misuse does not lend itself to a 'one-solution' approach. Consequently, a variety of treatment options are provided, including counselling and support, detoxification, treatment at therapeutic communities, needle exchange, and methadone maintenance. In practice, since the early 1990s, there has been an emphasis on methadone maintenance for opiate misusers, but more recently, rehabilitation has been increasingly stressed.[7]

---

7   The increased emphasis on rehabilitation in drug services in Ireland is reflected in the service plans produced by the ERHA, representing the three health board areas where the majority of drug users reside. The ERHA has also devised a rehabilitation/re-integration blueprint, to guide the development of rehabilitation services, and will be appointing three rehabilitation co-ordinators, to develop the rehabilitation aspect of drug treatment.

The treatment services aimed at drug users are organised at regional and local levels under the health boards and increasingly will involve more active liaison with local government structures. At present, the main funding comes through the Department of Health and Children to the health boards, and from them to voluntary and community agencies. Health boards are not consistent in the way they organise their drug treatment services. In some health board areas, drug services are provided under Health Promotion or Public Health, while, in others, services are provided under the Psychiatric Services umbrella.

Drug treatment services are provided through a network of treatment locations and the policy is to provide treatment locally where possible (Department of Health and Children, 2000b). Thus, in addition to some central treatment services, a network of addiction centres and satellite clinics has been developed, particularly in the ERHA area. Primary provision is also continually being developed and the involvement of general practitioners (GPs) and local pharmacies in local delivery is being encouraged.

Information on all those in treatment is collected on an anonymous basis by the DMRD of the HRB, through the National Drug Treatment Reporting System (NDTRS). Annual reports are produced (O'Brien, Moran, Kelleher & Cahill, 2000). Summary reports for different interest groups are planned for 2001.

Some recent initiatives in treatment policy and programmes and trends are outlined below in summary form.

Policy and Emerging Issues

- A review of the National AIDS Strategy has been carried out and the AIDS Policy 2000 was published in June 2000 (Department of Health and Children, 2000b).
- Hepatitis C is becoming an increasing problem amongst IDUs.
- Homelessness amongst drug misusers and former misusers is recognised as an increasing problem, not addressed adequately by existing treatment policy.
- As at October 2000, there is much media coverage and political concern regarding the 406 opiate addicts on the waiting list for treatment in clinics around Dublin.

Health Boards and Other Government Agencies

- All health boards have continued to expand their prevention, treatment and rehabilitation programmes. This is particularly so in the three health board areas covered by the ERHA, where the opiate problem is most acute.
- In 1999 and 2000 all health boards were provided with additional funding to continue to develop all aspects of their drug prevention and treatment services.

- The funding available to the EHB/ERHA to develop drug programmes and services has increased from IR£1million/€1.27 million in 1992, to IR£17 million/ /€21.6 million in 1999, and IR£22 million/€27.95 million in 2000.
- Increased resources were allocated in 1999 by central Government to all health boards to develop databases and information systems, to help characterise the drugs problem in their areas.
- The EHB published an 'Inventory of Policies' for its AIDS/drug addiction services in October 1998 (EHB, 1998). It covers policy in all main areas, under the headings treatment, viral illnesses, general and administrative.
- Three liaison midwives are to be appointed in the ERHA area to deal with pregnant misusers (one has already been appointed).
- The Irish Prisons Service and the ERHA have put together a joint programme to ensure greater cohesion and continuity of care in the treatment available to drug misusers entering and leaving prison.
- The ERHA has been reconceptualising its service provision and affording a greater role to prevention and rehabilitation, along with the traditional focus on treatment.
- In 1999 the EHB developed a Rehabilitation Blueprint, which realigns treatment services to have a rehabilitation focus. This new focus will commence at assessment stage.
- A rehabilitation co-ordinator will be appointed in each of the three health board areas covered by the ERHA.
- FÁS has allocated a significant number of Community Employment places to rehabilitation programmes for recovering drug misusers. These programmes are being developed through the LDTFs.

Primary Healthcare Providers and Community-Based Services

- The expansion of the provision of drug treatment services by means of the primary healthcare system continues for stabilised users.
- The Misuse of Drugs (Supervision of Prescription and Supply of Methadone) Regulations 1998 came into force in July 1998, imposing strict control on the prescribing and dispensing of methadone. The regulations aim, *inter alia*, to reduce the leakage of methadone onto the illicit market.
- In 1998 treatment cards were introduced for those receiving methadone.
- Five GP co-ordinators have been recruited to facilitate GP involvement in community-based drug treatment in the three area health boards covered by the ERHA, and to help shorten the waiting list. Liaison persons have been appointed in other health board areas.

- By the end of July 2000, there were 4,851 people receiving methadone in Ireland (only ninety of these were from outside of the ERHA area). In 1998 there had been 3,600 receiving methadone in the ERHA area (ERHA, personal communication).
- In August 2000 there were 158 GPs prescribing methadone, 131 of these in the ERHA area, leaving just 27 in the rest of the country. In addition, there were 207 pharmacists dispensing methadone to clients who were either attending a GP-based substitution programme or attending satellite clinics. Of the 207 pharmacists dispensing methadone, 154 were located in the ERHA area (ERHA, personal communication).
- Needle exchange has been available in the Dublin area since 1989. There were 6,000 people attending needle exchange programmes in the EHB area in 1999 (the figure for 2000 is not available). The DMRD is exploring the possibility of reporting on these statistics, along with the regular drug treatment figures in the NDTRS.
- There is anecdotal evidence that benzodiazepine misuse has increased, as has the prescribing of benzodiazepine by a small number of GPs. A committee to examine the nature and extent of benzodiazepine prescribing in Ireland has been established by the Department of Health and Children. The committee will make recommendations on good prescribing practice in general, and in particular in relation to the management of drug misusers.
- Public opposition to the opening of clinics in neighbourhoods continues. The health boards are adopting a partnership approach with local communities. The ERHA Service Plan for the AIDS/Drugs Service includes a commitment to 'Social Development'.

Evaluation

There has been very little work done on the evaluation of drug treatment services to date. However, a culture of evaluation is beginning to develop within the health services.

In 1999 a review of the EHB's AIDS/drug addiction services was conducted (Farrell, Gerada & Marsden, 2000). The purpose of the review was to:

- appraise the current drugs policies and practices within the service;
- examine the development of the service since the last review, conducted five years earlier; and
- comment on the EHB service response, in the context of trends and practices elsewhere.

One performance indicator for drug-treatment centres that the report investigated was the results of urine tests for opiates, benzodiazepines and tricyclics from five addiction clinics across the EHB area. These tests were conducted over a four-month period in 1999. The results indicated that, in aggregate, there was a 70 per cent reduction in heroin use among those attending for treatment. However, high rates of benzodiazepine use were found (65% positive), which suggests a major problem of polydrug use among drug users in treatment. The authors indicated that the costs of urine screening in EHB clinics were disproportionately high and needed to be reviewed. The review also found that a number of satellite clinics informally reported rates of returning to work among clients of 40 per cent (Farrell et al., 2000).

The report concluded that the EHB had succeeded in achieving a major expansion in services over the last five years and that the rates of opiate use, as indicated by urine testing, suggested that clinics were operating to a very high standard according to that particular parameter. The authors recommended that an audit of prescribing processes for benzodiazepine be conducted within the service as a matter of urgency. They also argued that the needle exchange service needed to be expanded and that services should be broadened to include briefer types of intervention.

Training

The need for training of personnel involved in the drug services requires further attention (see Section 7.10). Since the introduction of the Methadone Prescribing Protocol in 1998, GPs have been required to undergo specific training before they are permitted to prescribe methadone. The Irish College of General Practitioners provides this training, in conjunction with the relevant local health board. The training aims to provide GPs with the knowledge, skills and attitudes required to manage opiate misusers in general practice. There are two training levels, and the level attained will dictate the nature of the contract the GP will have with the health board in terms of the substitution service he/she can provide in the general-practice setting.

- Level 1 permits GPs to prescribe methadone only for clients who have been stabilised on a methadone programme in a clinic. These stabilised clients are referred to the GP from the health board treatment centres. GPs in this group are limited to providing services for a maximum of fifteen clients.

- Level 2 permits GPs to initiate the treatment of opiate-dependent persons. Doctors must have worked for a minimum of one year in a clinic before they can undergo this training. A GP in this group may treat up to thirty-five clients in his/her own practice, but, if in a practice with two or more doctors, may cater for a maximum of fifty clients.

In an effort to ensure comprehensive national epidemiological information on treated drug misuse, the DMRD makes an input, on the completion of NDTRS forms, into the content of the Irish College of General Practitioners' training. Individual training is also provided by the DMRD for those who complete NDTRS forms.

7.5.2 Substitution Programmes

The objectives of substitution programmes vary depending on the type of programme. While the ultimate aim of the services is to facilitate the individual's return to a drug-free lifestyle, a variety of programmes are available. Some programmes aim to detoxify the individual on a short-term programme, while others offer longer-term maintenance, which is not subject to a specific time limit.

Substitution programmes in Ireland are organised centrally. Therefore, a description will be given of the delivery and organisation of substitution services rather than a programme by programme approach, as taken in previous sections.

Admission to Substitution Programmes – During the early 1990s drug substitution services in Ireland were expanded and became more widely available to the opiate-using population. In accessing methadone maintenance programmes preference has always been given to pregnant women and those who have AIDS or are HIV positive. However, in 1998 the EHB produced an 'Inventory of Policies' which lays down criteria for admission to substitution programmes (EHB, 1998). These are as follows:

- clients must meet physical, emotional and behavioural criteria for addiction, as set down by the International Classification of Diseases Version 10 (ICD-10);
- clients must be 18 years of age. Those between the ages of 18 and 20 require a more extensive investigation before being commenced on methadone;
- the parents of clients under the age of 18 must attend and give parental consent. There should be a history of at least one failed detoxification, usually two or three, preferably at inpatient level. However, where patients have a very long history that can be verified, this condition may be waived;
- for admission to a maintenance programme, a client must have an extensive one-year history of intravenous drug use. For interim programmes a client must have been using opiates for a minimum of two years and/or injecting for one year; and
- clients must have gone through at least one previous detoxification attempt.

Special circumstances may dictate being accepted on a programme without fulfilling all the above criteria. Such circumstances include being HIV positive, being pregnant or being a partner of a client already on a programme.

Prior to the introduction of these guidelines, the criteria for admission onto maintenance programmes were generally left to the discretion of an individual GP or particular clinic. As such, there may have been extensive variation between programmes in terms of the criteria used for admission.

Prior to October 1998 there was no policy implementation in relation to GPs prescribing methadone. There are no data available on the extent to which GPs prescribed methadone up until this point, as the provision of such a service was at the discretion of individual GPs. However, in the early 1990s there was a move away from the centralised specialist model toward a more decentralised model of service provision. This called for the involvement of community-based GPs and pharmacists in the prescribing and dispensing of methadone. Although some individual GPs were already involved in providing this service, the aim was to establish a structured and co-ordinated approach to the provision of services. An Expert Group was set up to develop a suitable treatment protocol. In March 1993 the Protocol for the Prescribing of Methadone was issued, setting out guidelines for GPs prescribing methadone within the general-practice setting, and for pharmacists in their dispensing of methadone (Department of Health, 1993). Guidelines, set out in a review of this protocol (Department of Health, 1997), were implemented in October 1998. Consequently, the Misuse of Drugs (Supervision of Prescription and Supply of Methadone) Regulations were drawn up in 1998.

The guidelines aim to create a more controlled environment for the prescribing and dispensing of methadone. Under the Regulations the prescribing medical practitioner must register each client in receipt of a methadone prescription on the Central Treatment List. The guidelines aim to restrict the number of clients for whom individual GPs can prescribe methadone. While there is no specific licence required by GPs in Ireland to provide substitution programmes, they are required to undergo training and must be approved by the relevant health board. Methadone itself is a licensed prescription drug controlled under Schedule 2 of the Misuse of Drugs Regulations, 1988. Methadone is currently prescribed in two service settings: clinic setting and GP setting. Furthermore, it is also dispensed from community pharmacies.

Clinics – Clinics have been developed specifically to meet the needs of drug users. Expansion in clinic services has been overwhelmingly in the area of substitution programmes, including methadone detoxification, stabilisation and maintenance. The number of clinics where methadone is prescribed has grown from two in 1991 to four in 1994, to forty-five in 1999 and fifty-three in 2000. Forty-nine of the fifty-three clinics are based in the ERHA area, where the large majority of opiate users reside.

Clinics fall into one of two categories. First is the category referred to as 'addiction centres', where a range of services are available to clients, including substitution programmes. The majority of the clients attending these clinics are dispensed their methadone on-site on a daily basis; this means they consume the methadone under the supervision of a member of staff. Supervised urine samples are taken on a regular basis. When clients have demonstrated a certain level of stability, by providing opiate-negative samples over a period of time, they may be dispensed 'take home' doses. This requires less frequent attendance at the clinic.

The second category of clinic is referred to as the 'satellite clinic'. These are clinics based in communities identified as having a significant opiate-using population. These clinics provide methadone-prescribing services, although it is not dispensed on site. Rather, clients attend a designated community pharmacy where their methadone is dispensed.

General Practitioners – As mentioned above, in 1993 a protocol was published for the prescribing of methadone in the general-practice setting. The basic premise outlined in the 1993 protocol was that GPs should take on responsibility for the care of opiate-dependent people once they had been stabilised in either an addiction centre or a satellite clinic. GPs and clients should then have the continued support of that centre or clinic. In 1997 a protocol review committee produced a report (Department of Health, 1997), the recommendations of which were implemented in October 1998. The main changes this has had on the organisation and delivery of methadone services in the general-practice context are:

- GPs have to register with the health board to enable them to prescribe methadone;
- GPs are restricted in the number of drug users they may treat, depending on their level of training;
- only GPs who have undergone specialised training may initiate the prescription of methadone in the treatment of drug addiction. Other GPs may only treat those already stabilised in a clinic setting;
- GPs are no longer allowed to prescribe methadone to patients in a private capacity but have to provide the service free of charge to the patient; and
- all patients in receipt of a methadone prescription have to be registered on a Central Treatment List.

As with the number of clinics providing substitution services, the number of GPs offering the service has increased dramatically over recent years. In 1996 there were 58 GPs registered as prescribing methadone in their practice setting; this grew to 97 in 1998, 143 in 1999 and in 2000 has grown to 158.

Community Pharmacists – As substitution programmes have become more decentralised, the role of the community pharmacist has become increasingly important. Pharmacies are responsible for dispensing methadone to clients attending a GP-based substitution programme and those attending satellite clinics. Each client is assigned to a particular pharmacy in the local community, from which his or her methadone will be dispensed. Pharmacists are involved in dispensing take-home doses and also provide a supervised administration service. The Pharmaceutical Society of Ireland recommends that pharmacists agree a written contract with clients when initiating these services. Contracts detail the pharmacy service and the expected standard of behaviour of clients. The number of pharmacies involved in dispensing methadone has increased significantly over recent years. As of 2000 there were 207 pharmacists involved in dispensing methadone; 154 of these were based in the ERHA area (Pharmaceutical Society of Ireland, personal communication).

It is required that methadone be prescribed using special prescription forms. These prescription forms must be correctly written and allow for a single supply or supply on installment. The prescription form must also indicate whether or not the administration of the dose should be supervised by the pharmacist (Department of Health, 1997).

Substitution Drugs – The only substitution drug currently prescribed in Ireland is oral methadone. Prior to 1996 the only form of methadone available in Ireland was Physeptone Linctus (2mg methadone per 5ml of syrup). As part of a reorganisation of the methadone treatment services, the regional health boards decided to transfer patients onto methadone mixture (5mg methadone per 5ml of syrup). This change was first implemented in treatment clinics and then in general-practice surgeries. This methadone mixture is the only form currently available from treatment services.

The Pharmaceutical Society of Ireland has proposed the use of non-opioid alternatives to methadone, such as Lofexidine, for the management of addiction and this is currently being reviewed. Research projects under the management of the consultant psychiatrist with responsibility for drug misuse in the Northern Area Health Board of the ERHA, Dr Brian Sweeney, are also currently investigating the effectiveness of Lofexidine, LAAM and Bupenorphine.

No research has been carried out to date in Ireland into the extent to which substitution drugs are diverted. However, NDTRS data show that of those who presented to drug-treatment services with problem drug use during 1998 (N=5,076), 6.3 per cent reported 'street methadone' as their main drug of misuse. This suggests that at the time, methadone continued to be diverted from the treatment services. However, it will be necessary to examine these figures as they become available, to assess the impact of the tighter regulations surrounding methadone prescribing on the diversion of methadone to the street market.

Additional Services – Counselling is available on site to those attending a clinic-based programme. Interim programmes have counsellors available to clients on an *ad hoc* basis. Access to counselling is provided where there are complex/acute issues involved. Clients of maintenance programmes are allocated a full-time counsellor. Although counselling is recommended while participating in the programme, it is ultimately voluntary. In the general-practice setting clients can be referred to local counsellors if so required. Attendance is also voluntary. There are no data available on the level of uptake of counselling services or the number of visits made per client from either treatment setting.

Both clinic and general-practice programmes require clients to give regular, supervised urine samples, which are tested for the presence of prohibited substances. In the clinics, urine samples are taken on a twice-weekly basis during stabilisation, and on at least a weekly basis once clients are stabilised. These samples are all screened for opiates and methadone. On a monthly basis all clients are screened for other substances such as benzodiazepines and cocaine. Where clients are identified as having a specific 'problem' with such substances, they are screened for them on at least a weekly basis. Where clients are transferred to a general-practice programme, urine screening is organised between the health board and the GP and is carried out on a weekly basis.

Research and Data Available on Substitution Programmes – At the end of July 2000 there were 4,851 clients receiving substitution treatment in Ireland. Clients of both general-practice and clinic-based programmes are all registered on a Central Treatment List. As mentioned earlier, opiate use in Ireland is overwhelmingly based in the ERHA area, and therefore most substitution programme clients are resident there. As of July 2000 only 90 of a total of 4,851 clients registered on the Central Treatment List were receiving substitution services outside the ERHA area. Data gathered through the Central Treatment List are confidential and are not available for epidemiological analysis.

Most research carried out in Ireland with clients of substitution programmes has focused on their identity as IDUs rather than on their experiences of substitution programmes. In addition, the research has been limited to sample populations from one particular clinic (Smyth, Keenan & O'Connor, 1995; Dorman, Keenan, Schuttler, Merry & O'Connor, 1997; Smyth *et al.*, 1998; Williams, O'Connor & Kinsella, 1990). Little research has been done on substitution programmes *per se*.

A nation-wide general population survey on drug-related knowledge, attitudes and beliefs in Ireland (Bryan, Moran, Farrell & O'Brien, 2000), known as KAB1, was carried out by the DMRD of the HRB. In this study 1,000 members of the public were asked about a range of drug-related issues, including drug treatment services. In relation to substitution services, respondents were asked to what extent they agreed with the following statement:

> Medically prescribed heroin substitutes (such as methadone/physeptone) should be available to drug addicts.

Only 16.1 per cent disagreed with this statement while 63.5 per cent agreed and 20.3 per cent responded 'don't know'. These views appear to contradict the negative attitudes expressed by communities in relation to the establishment of treatment centres in their localities.

7.6 After-Care and Re-Integration

There has been an increased focus on rehabilitation in recent years, as indicated by recent speeches of the Minister of State for Local Development with Special Responsibility for the National Drugs Strategy, the service plans of the ERHA, and their development of a rehabilitation/re-integration blueprint. However, as yet, there are relatively few rehabilitation programmes in place. Both statutory and community agencies provide these services. Below are some examples of the types of rehabilitation programmes available.

St Francis Farm has been established by Merchant's Quay, a voluntary drug-treatment project, based in Dublin. St Francis Farm is an innovative, drug-free therapeutic training facility situated in a rural area in the south-east of Ireland. It offers a one-year programme for former drug users, involving both vocational and educational training in a farm environment. Participants learn a wide range of skills including animal care, horticultural techniques, catering and food preparation, building and joinery, machine maintenance and literacy/numeracy skills. Organic farming methods are used on the farm to mirror the chemical-free status of participants. The programme enables those with a low skill level to discover new areas of ability, which will help them to gain access to more formal training on completion of the programme.

Tallaght Rehabilitation Project was initiated in early 1997 and began to deliver services to drug users in the Tallaght area, one of Dublin's major suburbs, in February 2000. The project provides education and training to former drug users, and to drug users who have stabilised on a methadone maintenance programme. It is run by a management team of statutory and community representatives. The aim of the project is to facilitate drug users to re-integrate into their communities and into mainstream employment, education and training. Participants attend the project for four hours a day. This is broken down into three hours of education and training and one hour of social interaction and group work. Currently, fourteen participants, nine women and five men, are taking part in the programme.

Soilse, set up by the EHB in 1995, is a dedicated drug rehabilitation programme, specialising in insertion into employment, vocational training and education. Soilse aims to overcome the limitations of a psycho-therapeutic approach to addiction, by building goals and supporting participants in their desire to re-socialise themselves personally, economically and culturally. Soilse also seeks to re-integrate former drug users into society through restoring independence, self-esteem and self-direction. The programme is a non-residential day drug-rehabilitation model, balancing group therapy and counselling (resistance training and normative education) with creativity and soft vocation skills. An evaluation of the project has indicated that it has been successful in enhancing participants' self-esteem and in facilitating their entry to employment and training.

FÁS, the state training agency, has forged links with the LDTFs. Many participants taking part in LDTF rehabilitation programmes are doing so under the Community Employment Scheme operated by FÁS, which aims to facilitate the long-term unemployed in returning to work. FÁS is also making a substantial number of training slots available for drug addicts in treatment (Farrell *et al.*, 2000).

7.7 Interventions in the Criminal Justice System

This section describes the interventions put in place in the Irish criminal justice system, which aim to address the needs of drug-using offenders. The interventions correspond with the various stages at which the offender may be involved with the criminal justice system:

7.7.1 Alternatives to Custody
7.7.2 Garda Custody Interventions
7.7.3 Prison-Based Interventions
7.7.4 Post-Release Interventions

In addition, evaluations carried out on these interventions are discussed (Section 7.7.5) and drug-related training undertaken by those working in the criminal justice system described (Section 7.7.6).

7.7.1 Alternatives to Custody

The range of alternatives to custody available to offenders in the Irish criminal justice system are laid out in Chapter 2 of this report. However, one intervention programme aimed specifically at drug-using offenders is detailed here. The **Bridge Project** is a community-based programme for young adult offenders, which provides an alternative to custody. Supported by the Probation and Welfare Services, it aims to prevent re-offending by young adult offenders (aged between 17 and 26 years), who would otherwise receive substantial custodial sentences. The programme addresses the key factors that contribute to and are associated with criminal behaviour, such as drug addiction. The programme consists of three phases.

- Phase 1 involves a detailed assessment of each participant, to determine his/her strengths and weaknesses, and prepares participants for the second stage of the project, which involves group work. During Phase 1, addictions and other personal and social problems are identified.

- Phase 2 consists of a seventeen-week, intensive group-based module, which focuses on participants' offending behaviour and how it has affected them, their families and the victims. Contributing factors that can influence offending behaviour, such as alcohol, drug and gambling addictions, family relationship problems, violence and anger management, are also addressed. During this phase, participants' education, training and work needs are assessed.

- Phase 3 supports participants in pursuing personal goals in education, training and employment. This phase continues until participants' court orders are completed.

An evaluation of the Bridge Project (Kelleher Associates, 1998) has shown that participants have responded positively to the programme.

7.7.2 Garda Custody Interventions

There are no specific interventions aimed at drug-using offenders when they are brought into custody. However, in Ireland, any individual held in custody in a Garda station has the right to request to see a GP (Criminal Justice Act, 1984 (Treatment of Persons in Custody in Garda Síochána Stations) Regulations, 1987). Where a drug user requests to see a GP, the GP may tend to the individual while she/he is being held in custody and will assess whether to provide the individual with medication, e.g. methadone, to alleviate withdrawal symptoms. However, data are not currently collected on either the number of people held in custody who avail of this service, or the proportion who do so as a consequence of their drug use.

7.7.3 Prison-Based Interventions

A number of prison-based interventions meet the needs of drug-using offenders. They include substitution programmes, education programmes and self-help groups.

On imprisonment there is a standard thirteen-day **methadone detoxification programme** offered to prisoners who are found to test positive for opiates. This service, however, is not available in all the country's prisons and tends to be based in the Dublin prisons. In what has been the main committal prison in Ireland up until recently (Mountjoy Prison, Dublin), there were an estimated 1,200 – 1,500 prisoners receiving methadone detoxification per year (Department of Justice, Equality and Law Reform, 1999). Prisoners who may have been stable on a methadone maintenance programme in the community are generally detoxified upon incarceration.

The following is the detoxification regime followed in Mountjoy Prison, Dublin. This is a methadone-based detoxification programme, in which Melleril[8] (25mg) is also offered for the first seven nights of detoxification. In Mountjoy Prison this programme has been described as being provided in an 'essentially unstructured and unsupervised fashion, with no follow-up or medium to long term planning' (Department of Justice, Equality and Law Reform, 1999). The programme is the same for each prisoner, irrespective of the quantity of opiates being used prior to imprisonment. The doses involved are as follows:

Day 1–2 25ml methadone mixture (green colour)
Day 3–4 20ml methadone mixture (green colour)
Day 5–8 15ml methadone mixture (green colour)
Day 9–11 10ml methadone mixture (green colour)
Day 12–13 5ml methadone mixture (green colour)
Melleril 25mg each night on days1–7 of the programme

The provision of methadone maintenance within the Irish prison system remains limited. Methadone maintenance is only available to prisoners who are HIV positive or

---

8   Melleril contains thioridazine, which belongs to the phenothiazine class of drugs. Among other uses, it is used to relieve tension and anxiety.

who have AIDS and, to a limited extent, to those who were on a maintenance programme prior to imprisonment. In a limited number of prisons, including the country's main male juvenile prison and main remand prison, a methadone maintenance programme is available to those prisoners coming from the community who are already on a methadone maintenance programme. This is a recent development in service provision. Drug testing is used to monitor prisoners receiving methadone on a maintenance basis in prison.

The Probation and Welfare Services provide a **Drug Awareness Programme** in a number of Dublin prisons. This is a four-week programme consisting of one session per week. The principal aim is to educate participants about their drug use and the associated risks. It is aimed at all prisoners with a history of drug use, including those who have ceased their drug use and those who are continuing to use in the prison setting. The programme is run regularly in a couple of prisons but staffing shortages prevent its being a more widespread service.

A seven-week **Drug Detoxification and Rehabilitation Programme** is run by Probation and Welfare officers in the Medical Unit of Mountjoy Prison. The programme caters for nine male prisoners at a time. There is no equivalent service available to female prisoners. To access the programme, prisoners are interviewed by Probation and Welfare officers and assessed for suitability. Only prisoners with less than twenty-six months to serve, or with a court sentence review date less than twenty-six months away, may apply for the programme. Participation entails an initial methadone detoxification, followed by an intensive rehabilitation programme. A multi-disciplinary team, including both medical staff and counsellors from outside agencies, delivers this programme. Participants who remain drug free during the seven-week period are then transferred to a designated drug-free unit (the Training Unit). While workers from a therapeutic community are involved in service provision for this particular programme, there is no therapeutic community programme available to drug users in the Irish prison system. A similar programme, with greater focus on factors associated with imminent release into the community, is run over an eleven-week period. This is also based in Mountjoy Prison, Dublin, and will be discussed in the post-release section (7.7.4) below.

Prisoners may also access **self-help groups** while incarcerated. However, the only structured self-help group available to prisoners that specifically addresses the issue of drug use is Narcotics Anonymous (NA).

There is a **designated drug-free unit** (the Training Unit) in Mountjoy Prison, Dublin, where a limited number of prisoners are able to serve their sentence. The drug-free status of the unit is monitored by randomised drug testing, which all prisoners, irrespective of whether they have a drug-using history or not, are required to undergo. When a prisoner tests positive for a prohibited substance, he is moved either to another prison or to another area of Mountjoy.

7.7.4 Post-Release Interventions

In Ireland there is no formal referral scheme to treatment for drug-using prisoners on release. The need to develop a structured through-care programme from the prison system to the community has been identified within the Irish criminal justice system (Irish Prisons Service, 2000). The Probation and Welfare Services of the Department of Justice, Equality and Law Reform carry out group work programmes in the prison setting. These aim to promote desired behavioural changes in terms of risk behaviour and drug addiction, and to help prisoners cope with imprisonment and to prepare them for life demands following release from prison.

There are also a couple of specific projects under way that are targeted at dealing with the issues surrounding release.

The Probation and Welfare Service of Mountjoy Prison, Dublin, runs an eleven-week **Drug Rehabilitation Programme** that focuses on factors associated with imminent release into the community. The programme facilitates prisoners in developing a Community Release Plan through contact with their Probation and Welfare officer. After the initial eleven-week period, prisoners are released subject to Temporary Release Rules. Prisoners then contact their Probation and Welfare officer and link in with therapeutic, education, training and employment contacts in the community.

The **Cork LDTF** has established a rehabilitation programme for ex-prisoners. This project, based in Cork, received funding to set up a rehabilitation programme, with the aim of integrating ex-prisoners back into mainstream society and stopping them from re-offending. The project is managed by a partnership of voluntary and statutory bodies but has a specific management committee of four. The Probation and Welfare Services of the Department of Justice, Equality and Law Reform, the prison governor, his staff and the head teacher in the Education Department in Cork Prison, have been the primary animators in the development of this project. The project serves the inmates of the prison who, prior to detention, resided in the Cork LDTF area, but also works with family members of prisoners and with ex-prisoners and those who are on probation. An addiction counsellor has been employed by the project to work with the target group.

The project provides a counselling and referral service to clients referred by the Probation and Welfare Services. The project also provides an individual counselling service in Cork Prison and an Addiction Education and Awareness Programme. The worker who runs an Alcohol Management Course with the Intensive Probation Scheme also has links with the Auto Crime Diversion Unit. A working alliance has been established with a number of related groups. Since the project's inception, 181 people have had some form of contact with the counsellor. In addition to this number, there is a current waiting list of fifteen.

The **CONNECT Project** was established in Mountjoy Prison, Dublin, under the European DESMOS project, which is supported by the European Social Fund under the Integra Employment Initiative. The main objective of the CONNECT project is 'to encourage the (re) integration of offenders in society through employment as a support.' Each country has developed its own national programme, based on the guidelines on employment recommended by the Council of Europe. The guidelines have four aims:

- improving employability;
- developing entrepreneurship;
- encouraging adaptability of businesses and their employees; and
- strengthening the policies of equal opportunities for women and men.

In Mountjoy Prison, the CONNECT project is an action-research project, led by the Department of Justice, Equality and Law Reform and run by the National Training and Development Institute. Initially the project carried out research to identify gaps in education and training provision in Mountjoy Prison and the Training Unit. In response, the project developed and implemented pilot strategies and systems to fill the gaps identified and improve the employability of offenders while in custody. Included in the pre-vocational training is training in job-seeking skills and work-related social skills. The process at the centre of the project is described as the 'transition from custody, through training, on to reintegration in the community and more specifically, on to labour market participation'. Each course caters for up to fourteen male prisoners.

7.7.5 Evaluations of Interventions

There has been little evaluation of programmes aimed at drug users in the Irish criminal justice system. Crowley (1999) provided a medical review of the seven-week Drug Detoxification and Rehabilitation Programme in Mountjoy Prison, Dublin. Up to February 1999, 187 prisoners had entered the programme; 173 completed the detox; and 14 failed to complete the detox. While this implies a 93 per cent success rate, Crowley

(1999) highlighted the need for the success of this intervention to be determined by the six- and twelve-month relapse figures. Overall, it was found that there was a twelve-month relapse rate of 78 per cent. Crowley argued that while this might appear high, it compared favourably to outcome rates of other inpatient detoxification programmes.

7.7.6 Drug-Related Training for Staff

There is little specific training for those working in the Irish criminal justice system in relation to drug use and the specific needs of drug users.

As part of their training, members of An Garda Síochána (the Irish police force) receive instruction in the area of drug misuse. The programme includes training in:

- enforcement of drug-related laws;
- procedures for dealing with drug cases; and
- health and safety issues.

As part of its proposals for staff development, the Steering Group on Prison Based Drug Treatment Services (Irish Prisons Service, 2000) proposed that a special Prisons Service training officer be appointed. It is proposed that this training officer work in tandem with the ERHA's training department in the Drugs/AIDS Services. The officer would have responsibility for implementing a full training package for all staff in prisons who are working with drug users. The proposed training would comprise two levels. The first level would cover general education, basic skills training and awareness training of drug problems for all prison staff in relevant institutions. The second level would be more specific training for a core group of staff who would be working directly with drug users in prison treatment units.

7.8 Specific Targets and Settings

Projects dealing with gender-specific issues, minority groups and self-help groups are described below

The **SAOL programme**, based in Dublin, is an inner-city rehabilitation and training project for a small group of women in recovery or stabilised on methadone. It offers women a chance to acquire a range of skills, including literacy, numeracy and social skills, in order to give them a better opportunity to return to normal living. The project operates on principles derived from social justice, adult education and community development practice. An evaluation of the project found that women who participated in the programme reported increased stability in their lives, increased levels of self-esteem and gains in terms of educational and vocational development (SAOL Project, 1996).

Women's Health Project was established in the Baggot Street Clinic of the EHB, in Dublin, in 1991, to target women working in prostitution. The overall aims of the project are to prevent HIV and improve the general health and well-being of the women attending the project. There are two main components to the service: (1) a drop-in medical/counselling service in an informal setting, which aims to promote women's health in a confidential way, and (2) an outreach service. The project provides advice on safer sex and injecting, and needle exchange, and offers a wide range of health services including cervical smears, STD screening, contraception, HIV and hepatitis testing and referral to other services (O'Neill & O'Connor, 1999). The project operates on a peer-support basis, where women involved in prostitution contact other female sex workers (EMCDDA, 1999). Since May 1999 a harm-reduction service, consisting of a low dose of methadone and needle exchange, has been provided on a nightly basis from the EHB's mobile clinic (see Section 7.4.2). A welfare service is also available once a month, providing advice on welfare rights such as entitlements and housing.

Star Women's Rehabilitation Project, established in 1998, provides a fifty-week adult education and training course for fifteen women drug-users who have stabilised on methadone maintenance. It operates in the Ballymun area of Dublin. The programme consists of six-week modules, covering a variety of issues including communication, computers, team building, parenting, basic English, art drama and drug issues. Nine of the fifteen original cohort in the 1999 programme completed the course and went into either training or community employment or other employment. Of the six who did not complete the course, four also moved on to further positions or training. During the course of the year, many of the participants attained accredited training qualifications in fields such as word processing, addiction studies, childcare and youth studies.

Crèche, play-school and after-school facilities are provided in some local areas for the children of drug users receiving treatment. However, a study by Moran (1999) indicated that current levels of crèche provision were inadequate. The study found that only 20 per cent of drug-treatment centres in the Dublin area provided crèche facilities and that these existing crèche facilities were insufficient. The study found that lack of access to crèche facilities served as a barrier to treatment uptake.

Travellers Visibility Group, Cork LDTF, obtained funding to conduct research into the experiences and attitudes of young travellers and their families in relation to drug misuse. The Cork LDTF is developing focus groups among the young people, and through these groups it plans to assess drug experiences among the Traveller community.

The issue of drug use among ethnic minorities, including the indigenous Irish ethnic group known as 'travellers', is an emerging issue that requires further attention.

Self-help groups of various types are available through drug treatment centres. There are also a number of community-based self-help groups, including Narcotics Anonymous (NA), which is based on the twelve-step Alcoholics Anonymous (AA) philosophy, and Nar-Anon, a support group for the families and friends of drug users, based on similar principles.

7.9 Quality Assurance

A culture of evaluation is developing in the drugs area and is an integral aspect of programme development in some existing programmes. For example, guidelines have been developed for the conduct of evaluations in the context of the LDTFs (see Moran *et al.*, forthcoming).

Over 200 projects were funded through the LDTFs during 1999 and 2000. During April and May 2000, 133 of these projects were evaluated. The evaluations were process-oriented and centred on the development of objectives and the setting-up of appropriate structures and processes to support the achievement of these objectives rather than outcomes.

Of the projects evaluated, half were in the field of education and prevention, about a third (36%) in the field of treatment and rehabilitation projects, and the remainder were in the fields of education/prevention and treatment/rehabilitation (7%), research and information (3%) and supply control (3%). Most of the projects were based either in the voluntary/community sector (58%) or on a partnership between voluntary and statutory agencies (22%); 6 per cent were statutory agency projects; and the remaining 14 per cent were classified as 'other' (National Drugs Strategy Team, personal communication). On the basis of the evaluation reports produced, the National Drugs Strategy Team decided that 122 of the 133 projects would be mainstreamed. This means that these projects will receive statutory funding on an on-going basis in line with agreed procedures. A composite evaluation report is currently being compiled.

There is little evaluation carried out of treatment services but this is changing with a move towards evidence-based healthcare delivery. For example, a review of the EHB's AIDS/ drug addiction services was conducted during 1999 (Farrell *et al.*, 2000).

There is a need for far greater awareness of the value of evaluation. In addition, commitment by programme developers to evaluation work needs to be strengthened. Continuous provision of training is of vital importance in improving the quantity and quality of evaluations carried out in the drugs area.

7.10 Training

There has been a major proliferation in the number of training courses in the drugs area in Ireland in recent years. The growth in provision is partly in response to a growing demand for trained workers with expertise in the drugs area, e.g. community and voluntary sectors.

In August 1999 the Department of Tourism, Sport and Recreation commissioned a study to compile a directory of existing courses and to identify gaps and overlaps in training provision. The study identified a wide variety of training courses, ranging from single sessions to courses lasting between one and three years. The depth of coverage of the issues varies considerably, according to the length of the course and the level at which it is aimed. There are also variations in the training methods and in the underlying principles and approaches to the issue of drug misuse: the problem of drug misuse provokes different feelings, attitudes and beliefs, and these are reflected, to some extent, in the training courses listed in the directory. Some courses cover a wide variety of viewpoints, while others are clearly based in the context of a particular perspective. The directory is very extensive (although it claims not to be exhaustive) and includes an outline of almost forty courses (Department of Tourism, Sport and Recreation, 1999).

The courses listed in the directory are divided into six categories, according to course length and purpose:

a) short courses aimed at providing basic information and/or raising awareness of drug misuse among the general public;
b) short courses aimed at providing information, raising awareness and developing skills among those whose paid or voluntary work brings them into contact with drug misuse;
c) longer courses aimed at providing information, raising awareness and developing skills among those whose paid or voluntary work brings them in contact with drug misuse;
d) courses leading to professional qualifications in the field of drug misuse;
e) in-service training for professionals and other vocational groups working in the field of drug misuse or related areas; and
f) courses in drug misuse aimed at young people.

While there is a wide range of courses available, not all of these are available throughout the country. In general, the Dublin area is best provided for, while the range of training available elsewhere is more limited. However, there are indications that this is beginning to change.

7.11 Dissemination of Information on Demand Reduction

Dissemination of information on demand reduction activities in Ireland has been quite poor to date. The following developments will facilitate information exchange in the area.

A new **National Documentation Centre** is being established in the DMRD of the HRB. This new national resource, established under the National Advisory Committee on Drugs (NACD), will provide a major source of information on literature in the drugs misuse area in Ireland to interested individuals and agencies. This development will include the creation of a bibliographical database of research in this area, an annual inventory of current research and the establishment of an electronic library containing full text copies of research reports and other material that will be made available to users of the Documentation Centre. The Centre will also collaborate with EMCDDA in the development of its 'virtual library' project.

DrugNet Ireland is a newsletter compiled and distributed, free of charge, by the DMRD of the HRB[9] twice yearly. This magazine fulfils an important role in the distribution of information, news and research among health professionals and other interested parties involved in the drugs area in Ireland. Its readership includes community groups, policy makers, academics, treatment providers and educationalists. The newsletter contains information on demand reduction activities and includes information on ongoing research in drug misuse, recently published materials and reviews, recent and upcoming events, developments in the EU, local and world news, and information on research funding and fellowships. DrugNet Ireland can be downloaded electronically from the DMRD webpages on www.hrb.ie

EDDRA, the electronic databank described in Section 7.3.6, also plays a role in the dissemination of demand reduction information. During 2000 an EDDRA brochure, describing the facility, was developed and distributed with DrugNet Ireland, and at various seminars, workshops and conferences attended by members of the DMRD. In addition, a training session on evaluation was conducted by the DMRD with regional drug co-ordinators, among others, in attendance.

---

9   Contact Paul Cahill at the DMRD in the HRB.

It is hoped that the additional funding provided by the Department of Health and Children in 1999 to all health boards to develop databases and information systems will lead to the development of an inventory of projects and increase awareness of demand reduction projects under way in Ireland. At present the regional drugs co-ordinators are the repository of such information on demand reduction activities in the regional health board areas.

7.12 Conclusions

This chapter has provided an overview of demand reduction activities in the Irish context. Increased funding in recent years has led to heightened activity in the demand reduction area. It is important to note that many of the projects described have not been formally evaluated and thus can be of limited use in future planning. Evaluation needs to be an integral aspect of programme planning and development in the drugs area in the future. A culture of evaluation within the drugs services needs to be fostered.

7.13 References

Ballymun Local Drug Task Force (2000). 'Star Women's Rehabilitation Project'. Report commissioned by the National Drugs Strategy Team. Unpublished report. Dublin: Ballymun Local Drug Task Force.

Bowden, M. (1997). *Community Addiction Response Programme CARP – Killinarden: Review and interim evaluation report.* Dublin: Community Addiction Response Programme.

Bowden, M. (1998). *Review of the 'Copping On' Crime Awareness Initiative.* Dublin: The Children's Research Centre, Trinity College.

Bryan, A., Moran, R., Farrell, E. & O'Brien, M. (2000). *Drug-Related Knowledge, Attitudes and Beliefs in Ireland: Report of a nation-wide survey.* Dublin: The Health Research Board.

Burtenshaw, R. & O'Reilly, K. (2000). 'A Project Report on the Cabra Resource Centre'. Unpublished report. Dublin: Finglas/Cabra Local Drug Task Force.

Cox, G. & Lawless, M. (2000). *Making Contact: An evaluation of a syringe exchange.* Dublin: Merchant's Quay Project.

Crowley, D. (1999). The drug Detox Unit at Mountjoy Prison – A review. *The Journal of Health Gain, 3,* (3).

Department of Health (1993). *Report of the Expert Group on the Establishment of a Protocol for the Prescribing of Methadone.* Dublin: Department of Health.

Department of Health (1997). *Report of the Methadone Treatment Services Review Group.* Dublin: Department of Health.

Department of Health and Children (2000a). *The National Health Promotion Strategy 2000 – 2005.* Dublin: Department of Health and Children.

Department of Health and Children (2000b). *AIDS Strategy 2000 – Report of the National AIDS Strategy Committee.* Dublin: The Stationery Office.

Department of Justice, Equality and Law Reform (1999). 'Drug Misuse and Drug Treatment in the Prison System: Draft action plan'. Unpublished. Dublin: Department of Justice, Equality and Law Reform.

Department of Tourism, Sport and Recreation (1999). *Directory of Training Courses in Drug Misuse.* Dublin: Department of Tourism, Sport and Recreation.

Dorman, A., Keenan, E., Schuttler, C., Merry, J. & O'Connor, J. (1997). HIV risk behaviour in Irish intravenous drug users. *Irish Journal of Medicine, 166,* (4), 235–238.

Eastern Health Board (1998). *AIDS/Drug Addiction Services: Inventory of policies.* Dublin: Eastern Health Board.

EMCDDA (1996). *Annual Report on the State of the Drugs Problem in the European Union 1996.* Luxembourg: Office for Official Publications of the European Communities.

EMCDDA (1999). *Insights: Outreach work among drug users in Europe.* Luxembourg: Office for Official Publications of the European Communities.

Farrell, M., Gerada, C. & Marsden, J. (2000*).* 'External Review of Drug Services for "The Eastern Health Board"'. Unpublished Report. Dublin: Eastern Health Board.

Gallagher, C. (1999). 'A Qualitative Study to Assess the Impact on Parents Resulting from Their Involvement with the Fás le Chéile Project'. Unpublished Report.

Harding, S. (2000). Dublin Safer Dance Initiative: The 'Staying Alive' campaign. In E. Kiely & E. Egan (eds) *Harm Reduction: An information and resource booklet for agencies engaged in drug education.* Cork: Department of Applied Social Studies, National University of Ireland, Cork.

Irish Prisons Service (2000). *Report of the Steering Group on Prison Based Drug Treatment Services.* Dublin: Irish Prisons Service.

Kelleher Associates (1998). *The Employment and Education Services of the Bridge Project. A non-custodial alternative to prison.* An Interim Report. Dublin: Kelleher Associates.

Kiely, E. & Egan, E. (eds) (2000). *Harm Reduction : An information and resource booklet for agencies engaged in drug education.* Cork: Department of Applied Social Studies, National University of Ireland, Cork.

Moran, R. (1999). *The Availability, Use and Evaluation of the Provision of Crèche Facilities in association with Drug Treatment.* Dublin: The Health Research Board.

Moran, R., Dillon, L., O'Brien, M., Mayock, P. & Farrell, E. (forthcoming). *A Collection of Papers on Drug Issues in Ireland: Implementation of drug strategy, drug-related infectious diseases, cocaine use and women, children and drug use.* Dublin: Drug Misuse Research Division, The Health Research Board.

Morgan, M. (1997a). 'North Eastern Health Board – Healthy Schools Project: evaluation report'. Unpublished Report.

Morgan, M. (1997b & 2000). 'Crinan Project – evaluations'. Unpublished Reports.

Morgan, M. (1998). 'The Substance Abuse Prevention Programme: A formative evaluation.' Unpublished Report. Dublin: Department of Education and Science.

Morgan, M., Morrow, R., Sheehan, A. M. & Lillis, M. (1996). Prevention of substance misuse: Rationale and effectiveness of the programme 'On My Own Two Feet'. *Oideas, 44,* 5–25.

National Co-ordinating Committee on Drug Misuse (1991). *Government Strategy to Prevent Drug Misuse.* Dublin: The Department of Health.

NDP (2000). *Ireland, National Development Plan 2000 – 2006.* Dublin: The Stationery Office.

O'Brien, M., Moran, R., Kelleher, T. & Cahill, P. (2000). *National Drug Treatment Reporting System: Statistical bulletin 1997 and 1998.* Dublin: The Health Research Board.

O'Neill, M. & O'Connor, A. M. (1999). *Drug Using Women in Prostitution.* Dublin: Eastern Health Board.

O'Rourke, S. (2000). 'Jobstown Assisting Drug Dependency (JADD): Project report'. Unpublished Report.

Ruddle, H. (1993). 'Cork Social and Health Education Project. Strengthening Family Communication to Prevent Misuse of Alcohol and Drugs: An evaluation study'. Unpublished Report.

SAOL Project (1996). *An Interim Evaluation of the SAOL Project.* Dublin: SAOL.

Smyth, R., Keenan, E. & O'Connor, J. (1995). Hepatitis C infection among injecting drug users attending the National Drug Treatment Centre. *Irish Journal of Medical Science, 164,* (6), 267–268.

Smyth, R., Keenan, E. & O'Connor, J. (1998). Bloodborne viral infection in Irish injecting drug users. *Addiction, 93,* (11), 1649–1656.

Williams, H., O'Connor J. & Kinsella, A. (1990). Depressive symptoms in opiate addicts on methadone maintenance. *Irish Journal of Psychological Medicine,* (7), 45–46.

RECOMMENDED STANDARDS FOR PROBLEM DRUG USE PREVALENCE ESTIMATION WORK IN IRELAND AND FOR THE REPORTING OF PREVALENCE ESTIMATES

In order to ensure quality of Prevalence Estimates of problem drug use and to avoid such estimates being misinterpreted or discussed out of context, it is proposed that the European Monitoring Centre for Drugs and Drug Addiction (EMCDDA) recommendations[1] be put forward as a standard to be adopted by the National Working Group Meeting[2], for prevalence estimation work in Ireland. These include that :

- Emergent estimates should be placed in context with other information about the nature and extent of drug use within the locality
- More than one estimate should always be provided and preferably such estimates should be based on different data sources i.e. the multi-method, multi-data source principle - *greater confidence can be placed on results if several indicators point in the same direction*

---

1   EMCDDA (1997). *Estimating the Prevalence of Problem Drug Use in Europe.* EMCDDA Scientific Monograph Series No 1. Luxembourg: Office for Official Publications of the European Communities; and EMCDDA (1999). *Extended Annual Report on the State of the Drugs Problem in the European Union 1999.* Luxembourg: Office for Official Publications of the European Communities.
2   Drug Misuse Research Division (2000). 'Irish National Workshop on Prevalence Estimates as an Indicator of Drug Misuse'. Unpublished document, February 2000. Dublin: The Health Research Board.

- Estimates should be reported with confidence intervals/ranges - *estimates need to be assessed in conjunction with the statistical uncertainty that is inherent in any estimate*
- The prevalence estimation method used should be fully described, including a critical assessment of its applicability within the project and the assumptions underlying the method should be made explicit
- Each data source used should be described, along with summary statistics such as age distribution and gender breakdown
- The description of the data and its context should be transparent enough to allow others to re-analyse the data and to judge whether or not the conclusions made, particularly the prevalence estimates, are valid.

APPENDIX 2

CENSUS OF POPULATION – IRELAND

TABLE 2.1.
Ireland. Census of Population 1996.

Age Group	Male	Female	Total
0 – 4 years	128,740	121,654	250,394
5 – 9 years	145,335	137,608	282,943
10 – 14 years	167,377	158,710	326,087
15 – 19 years	173,950	165,586	339,536
20 – 24 years	149,143	144,211	293,354
25 – 29 years	129,363	129,682	259,045
30 – 34 years	127,735	133,194	260,929
35 – 39 years	126,140	129,536	255,676
40 – 44 years	120,064	120,377	240,441
45 – 49 years	113,816	111,584	225,400
50 – 54 years	94,818	91,829	186,647
55 – 59 years	77,809	75,998	153,807
60 – 64 years	68,690	69,256	137,946
65 – 69 years	60,256	66,553	126,809
70 – 74 years	50,124	62,418	112,542
75 – 79 years	35,228	48,869	84,097
80 – 84 years	21,074	34,697	55,771
85 years & over	10,570	24,093	34,663
Total	1,800,232	1,825,855	3,626,087

Source: Central Statistics Office.

APPENDIX 3
STATISTICS – IRELAND

TABLE 3.1

Ireland 1990 – 1999. Drug-Related Deaths* from Drug Dependence and Opiate Poisoning. Numbers and Percentages.

		1990	1991	1992	1993	1994	1995	1996	1997**	1998**	1999**
All Ages	N	7	8	14	18	19	43	53	55	99	80
	%	100	100	100	100	100	100	100	100	100	100
All Ages (Dublin Only)	N	6	8	14	16	17	39	43	49	76	66
	%	86	100	100	89	89	86	81	89	77	83
Gender	%M	86	100	79	89	95	86	83	87	76	74
	%F	14	0	21	11	5	14	17	13	24	24
Under 30 Years Old	N	7	4	8	8	11	22	30	34	53	35
	%	100	50	61	44	58	51	57	62	54	44
15–49 Years Old	N	7	7	14	16	19	39	50	52	90	70
	%	100	88	100	89	100	91	94	96	91	88
Drug Dependence (ICD-9 Code 304) (All Ages)	N	4	5	13	13	15	38	42	43	90	75
	%	57	63	93	72	79	88	79	78	91	94

* For the purpose of this report, a drug-related death is defined as one where the underlying or external cause of death was due to drug dependence (ICD-9 Code 304) or opiate poisoning (ICD-9 Code 965.0).
** Provisional data.

TABLE 3.2

Ireland 1982 – 1999. AIDS Cases and Deaths by Risk Category. Numbers.

Risk Category	1982 – 1992		1993		1994		1995		1996		1997		1998		1999	
	Cases	Deaths	Cases	Deaths	Cases	Deaths	Cases	Deaths	Cases	Deaths	Cases	Deaths	Cases	Deaths	Cases	Deaths
Intravenous Drug Use Related	142	61	43	21	22	27	25	27	34	17	10	1	12	8	16	7
Homo/Bisexual	109	45	13	14	27	11	16	11	34	16	12	3	13	9	13	5
Haemophiliacs/ Heterosexuals/ Others	52	27	12	9	18	6	13	8	11	1	8	2	14	4	11	5
Undetermined	5	3	0	0	0	0	1	0	0	0	2	1	2	0	1	0
Total	308	136	68	44	67	44	55	46	79	34	32	7	41	21	41	17

TABLE 3.3

Ireland 1994 – 1999. All and First Admissions to Inpatient Psychiatric Hospitals. All Ages. Numbers, Percentages and Rates.

Admissions	1995		1996		1997		1998		1999	
	All	First	All	First	All	First	All	First	All	First
Drug-Related Admissions (N)	580	172	678	263	691	280	846	308	893	354
Admissions for All Disorders (N)	26,440	7,246	26,656	7,130	26,069	7,049	25,295	7,137	25,118	7,147
Drug-Related (%) (Primary or Secondary Diagnosis)	2.2	2.4	2.5	3.7	2.7	4.0	3.3	4.3	3.6	5.0
Rate per 100,000	16.2	4.7	18.7	7.2	19.1	7.7	23.3	8.5	24.6	9.8

APPENDIX 4

EMCDDA STANDARD TABLES

TABLE 4.1
Population Surveys on Drug Use. Results, Study Details and Definitions
Survey of Lifestyle, Attitudes and Nutrition (SLÁN). Prevalence

Empty Cells indicate 'no information available'

COUNTRY Ireland DRUGS (Important: see 'drug definitions' in the Methodology box.)	All Adults 18-64			Young Adults 18-34			LIFETIME PREVALENCE (%) Broad Age Groups 18-24			25-34			35-44			45-54			55-64		
	M	F	T	M	F	T	M	F	T	M	F	T	M	F	T	M	F	T	M	F	T
1. Any Illegal Drugs	11.0	6.3	8.5	18.3	9.5	13.4	23.2	12.9	17.9	13.6	7.1	9.8	7.2	4.1	5.5	4.7	3.4	4.1	2.8	2.6	2.7
2. Cannabis	23.1	16.5	19.9	36.7	24.6	30.0	37.9	29.1	33.4	35.5	21.6	27.4	21.3	14.6	17.6	12.0	5.1	8.8	3.1	1.0	2.1
3. Opiates (Total)																					
4. Heroin																					
5. Other Opiates (Specify)																					
6. Cocaine (Total, including Crack)																					
8. Amphetamines																					
9. Ecstasy																					
10. Hallucinogens (Total)																					
11. LSD																					
12. Other Hallucinogens (Specify)																					
13. Hypnotics and Sedatives (Total)																					
14. Benzodiacepines																					
15. Other Medic. (Specify)																					
16. Solvents																					
17. Steroids																					
18. Other (Specify)																					

M = Male; F = Female; T= Total

TABLE 4.1 *contd.*

COUNTRY Ireland

LAST 12 MONTHS PREVALENCE (%)

DRUGS (Important: see 'drug definitions' in the Methodology box.)	All Adults 18-64			Young Adults 18-34			Broad Age Groups 18-24			25-34			35-44			45-54			55-64		
	M	F	T	M	F	T	M	F	T	M	F	T	M	F	T	M	F	T	M	F	T
1. Any Illegal Drugs																					
2. Cannabis	11.9	7.3	9.4	22.9	13.4	17.7	30.3	21.9	26.0	15.7	7.5	10.9	4.5	2.2	3.2	1.9	1.4	1.7	0.5	0.5	0.5
3. Opiates (Total)	0.4	0.1	0.2	0.8	0.2	0.5	0.7	0.4	0.5	0.9	0.1	0.4	0.0	0.0	0.0	0.0	0.0	0.0	0.0	0.0	0.0
4. Heroin	0.5	0.2	0.3	1.1	0.3	0.7	0.9	0.6	0.8	1.2	0.1	0.6	0.0	0.0	0.0	0.0	0.0	0.0	0.0	0.0	0.0
5. Other Opiates (Specify)	0.2	0.0	0.1	0.5	0.2	0.3	0.5	0.2	0.3	0.6	0.0	0.3	0.0	0.0	0.0	0.0	0.0	0.0	0.0	0.0	0.0
5. Cocaine (Total, including Crack)	1.9	0.8	1.3	4.1	1.5	2.6	4.9	2.1	3.4	3.3	1.1	2.0	0.2	0.0	0.1	0.0	0.0	0.1	0.0	0.0	0.0
8. Amphetamines	3.7	1.5	2.6	8.2	3.1	5.4	11.7	6.1	8.8	4.9	1.0	2.6	0.5	0.0	0.2	0.3	0.3	0.3	0.0	0.0	0.0
9. Ecstasy	3.0	1.8	2.4	6.5	3.6	4.9	9.6	6.7	8.1	3.7	1.4	2.4	0.5	0.1	0.2	0.3	0.3	0.4	0.0	0.0	0.0
10. Hallucinogens (Total)	2.1	0.4	1.4	4.6	1.4	2.8	7.6	2.4	4.9	1.9	0.8	1.2	0.4	0.3	0.3	0.0	0.1	0.1	0.0	0.0	0.0
11. LSD	2.0	0.9	1.4	4.3	1.8	2.9	6.3	3.1	5.1	1.5	0.9	1.1	0.2	0.3	0.2	0.0	0.1	0.1	0.0	0.0	0.0
12. Other Hallucinogens (Specify)	2.3	0.6	1.4	5.0	1.1	2.8	8.0	1.6	4.7	2.3	0.7	1.3	0.3	0.3	0.3	0.0	0.1	0.1	0.0	0.0	0.0
13. Hypnotics and Sedatives (Total)	1.3	1.2	1.2	1.8	1.1	1.4	2.7	1.6	2.1	1.0	0.7	0.8	0.5	0.8	0.7	1.2	2.2	1.7	1.1	1.2	1.1
14. Benzodiacepines																					
15. Other Medic. (Specify)																					
16. Solvents	0.5	0.2	0.3	1.2	0.4	0.8	1.8	1.0	1.4	0.6	0.0	0.3	0.0	0.0	0.0	0.0	0.0	0.0	0.0	0.0	0.0
17. Steroids																					
18. Other (Specify)																					

M = Male; F = Female; T = Total

TABLE 4.1 *cont'd.*

COUNTRY Ireland DRUGS (Important: see 'drug definitions' in the Methodology box.)	LAST 30 DAYS PREVALENCE (%)																		
	All Adults 18-64			Young Adults 18-34			Broad Age Groups												
							18-24			25-34			35-44			45-54			55-64		
	M	F	T	M	F	T	M	F	T	M	F	T	M	F	T	M	F	T	M	F	T
1. Any Illegal Drugs																					
2. Cannabis	7.2	3.2	5.1	14.1	6.0	9.7	20.7	10.0	15.3	7.8	3.1	5.1	2.2	0.7	1.3	1.6	0.7	1.2	0.5	0.5	0.5
3. Opiates (Total)																					
4. Heroin																					
5. Other Opiates (Specify)																					
5. Cocaine (Total, including Crack)																					
8. Amphetamines																					
9. Ecstasy																					
10. Hallucinogens (Total)																					
11. LSD																					
12. Other Hallucinogens (Specify)																					
13. Hypnotics and Sedatives (Total)																					
14. Benzodiacepines																					
15. Other Medic. (Specify)																					
16. Solvents																					
17. Steroids																					
18. Other (Specify)																					

M = Male; F = Female; T = Total

TABLE 4.1 *cont'd.*

Study Details	
Reference:	SLAN (Survey of Lifestyle, Attitudes and Nutrition). Centre for Health Promotion Studies, NUI, Galway. Drug module of survey not published.
Year	1998
Single/Repeated Study	To be repeated, four years
Context (health/crime/drugs only…)	Health and lifestyle behaviours
Area Covered	National, Republic of Ireland
Age Range	18+ years
Data Collection	Procedure Postal, Self-Administered Questionnaire
Sample Size	10,415
Sampling Frame	Electoral Register
Sampling Procedures	Proportionate Random Sample based on Health Board population size, and urban/rural breakdown.
Oversampled Groups	None
Weighting Procedures	None
Response Rate	15-69 (M,F,T); 15-34 (M,F,T). Total n=6,539, 62.2%.

TABLE 4.1 *cont'd.*

Definitions Drugs Definitions:	Description of what is included in each drug category
1. Any Illegal Drugs	Tranquilisers or sedatives, amphetamine, LSD, cocaine, heroin, ecstasy, solvents, magic mushrooms
2. Cannabis	Marijuana or cannabis
3. Opiates (Total)	
4. Heroin Heroin	
5. Other Opiates (Specify)	
5. Cocaine (Total, including Crack)	Cocaine (coke, crack)
8. Amphetamines	Amphetamines
9. Ecstasy Ecstasy	(E, XTC)
10. Hallucinogens (Total)	LSD and magic mushrooms
11. LSD	LSD (acid, trips)
12. Other Hallucinogens (Specify)	Magic mushrooms (pucal, mushies)
13. Hypnotics and Sedatives (Total)	Tranquilisers or sedatives without prescription (barbs, downers, jellies)
14. Benzodiacepines	
15. Other Medic. (Specify)	
16. Solvents	Solvents (e.g. glue, gas)
17. Steroids	
18. Other (Specify)	

TABLE 4.2
Population Surveys on Drug Use. Results and Study Details
Drug-Related Knowledge, Attitudes and Beliefs in Ireland (KAB1). Prevalence

Empty Cells indicate 'no information available'

COUNTRY Ireland	LIFETIME PREVALENCE (%)																						
	All Adults			Young Adults			Broad Age Groups																
	18-64			18-34			18-24			25-34			35-44			45-54			55-64		
DRUGS (Important: see 'drug definitions' in the Methodology box.)	M	F	T	M	F	T	M	F	T	M	F	T	M	F	T	M	F	T	M	F	T
1. Any Illegal Drugs																					
2. Cannabis	17.5	10.9	14.2	28.7	23.3	26.2	32.3	32.3	32.3	23.6	16.0	19.6	12.9	5.4	9.0	9.2	4.9	6.7	4.7	0.0	2.6
3. Opiates (Total)																					
4. Heroin																					
5. Other Opiates (Specify)																					
5. Cocaine (Total, including Crack)																					
8. Amphetamines																					
9. Ecstasy																					
10. Hallucinogens (Total)																					
11. LSD																					
12. Other Hallucinogens (Specify)																					
13. Hypnotics and Sedatives (Total)																					
14. Benzodiacepines																					
15. Other Medic. (Specify)																					
16. Solvents																					
17. Steroids																					
18. Other (Specify)																					

M = Male; F = Female; T = Total
No information available on last 12 months or last 30 days prevalence.

TABLE 4.2 *cont'd.*

Study Details	
Reference:	Bryan,A., Moran,R., Farrell,E. and O'Brien,M. (2000) *Drug-Related Knowledge, Attitudes and Beliefs in Ireland.* Dublin: Health Research Board.
Year	1998
Single/Repeated Study	Ad hoc (to be repeated)
Context (health/ crime/drugs only. . .)	General Social Omnibus Survey
Area Covered	Ireland
Age Range	18 years and over
Data Collection	Procedure Questionnaire, face-to-face interview
Sample Size	1,000
Sampling Frame	Electoral Register
Sampling Procedures	Two-stage proportionate to size random sampling design
Oversampled Groups	None
Weighting Procedures	None
Response Rate 18+ (Total)	64.5%

TABLE 4.3

School Surveys on Drug Use. Results, Study Details and Definitions

Irish Health Behaviours in School Aged Children Survey (HBSC). Prevalence.

Empty Cells indicate 'no information available'

| COUNTRY Ireland DRUGS (Important: see 'drug definitions' in the Methodology box.) | LIFETIME PREVALENCE (%) | | | | | | | | | | | | | | |
| | Total Sample 9-17 | | | Age Groups 11-12 | | | 13-14 | | | 15-16 | | | 17 | | |
	M	F	T	M	F	T	M	F	T	M	F	T	M	F	T
1. Any Illegal Drugs	22.3	15.3	18.1	10.9	5.7	8.0	19.5	13.2	16.2	32.0	23.0	27.5	33.2	32.5	32.8
2. Cannabis	16.2	8.7	12.3	4.9	1.5	3.0	12.0	4.1	8.0	27.0	16.1	21.7	28.7	28.5	28.5
3. Opiates (Total)															
4. Heroin	2.4	0.3	1.3	2.1	0.2	1.0	1.8	0.3	1.0	2.8	0.3	1.8	3.8	0.4	2.2
5. Other Opiates (Specify)															
5. Cocaine (total, including crack)	2.9	1.7	2.3	3.2	1.8	2.4	2.4	1.6	2.0	3.0	1.5	2.2	4.8	2.1	3.5
8. Amphetamines	3.9	1.3	2.6	1.9	0.3	1.0	2.4	0.7	1.5	6.1	2.2	4.2	8.0	5.3	6.6
9. Ecstasy	3.3	0.6	2.1	2.3	0.2	1.2	2.4	0.2	1.3	4.3	1.3	2.8	6.8	4.3	5.7
10. Hallucinogens (Total)	6.8	2.0	4.4	3.8	0.5	2.0	5.2	1.6	3.4	10.3	3.3	6.9	10.0	4.9	7.5
11. LSD	3.6	0.9	2.3	2.0	0.3	1.1	2.6	0.4	1.5	5.1	1.7	3.4	8.4	2.5	5.5
12. Other Hallucinogens (Specify)	5.6	1.8	3.6	3.4	0.4	1.7	4.2	1.5	2.8	8.3	2.6	5.5	7.7	3.5	5.7
13. Hypnotics and Sedatives (Total)	3.2	2.4	2.8	2.2	0.7	1.4	2.4	3.0	2.7	4.5	3.2	3.9	4.2	3.2	3.7
14. Benzodiazepines															
15. Other Medic. (Specify)															
16. Solvents	11.5	8.3	9.9	5.9	2.9	4.3	12.4	9.2	10.7	14.5	11.4	13.0	14.4	13.7	14.2
17. Steroids															
13. Other															

M = Male; F = Female; T = Total

TABLE 4.3 *cont'd.*

COUNTRY Ireland DRUGS (Important: see 'drug definitions' in the Methodology box.)	LAST 12 MONTHS PREVALENCE (%)														
	Total Sample			Age Groups											
	9-17			11-12			13-14			15-16			17		
	M	F	T	M	F	T	M	F	T	M	F	T	M	F	T
1. Any Illegal Drugs	14.1	6.7	10.3	3.9	1.0	2.3	10.1	3.1	6.5	23.8	12.7	18.3	25.8	22.4	24.0
2. Cannabis															
3. Opiates (Total)															
4. Heroin															
5. Other Opiates (Specify)															
5. Cocaine (Total, including Crack)															
8. Amphetamines															
9. Ecstasy															
10. Hallucinogens (Total)															
11. LSD															
12. Other Hallucinogens (Specify)															
13. Hypnotics and Sedatives (Total)															
14. Benzodiacepines															
15. Other Medic. (Specify)															
16. Solvents															
17. Steroids															
13. Other															

M = Male; F = Female; T = Total

Appendix 4: EMCDDA Standard Tables

Table 4.3 *cont'd.*

LAST 30 DAYS PREVALENCE (%)

COUNTRY Ireland DRUGS (Important: see 'drug definitions' in the Methodology box.)	Total Sample 9-17			Age Groups 11-12			13-14			15-16			17		
	M	F	T	M	F	T	M	F	T	M	F	T	M	F	T
1. Any Illegal Drugs	12.8	7.4	10.0	6.9	3.4	5.0	11.9	6.8	9.3	18.0	10.8	14.4	15.0	13.4	14.3
2. Cannabis	8.9	3.1	5.9	2.3	0.5	1.3	7.1	1.5	4.3	15.3	5.7	10.5	11.6	10.4	11.0
3. Opiates (total)															
4. Heroin	1.8	0.1	0.9	1.7	0.1	0.8	1.4	0.2	0.8	1.9	0.1	1.0	3.4	0.4	2.0
5. Other Opiates (specify)															
5. Cocaine (total, including crack)	2.2	1.2	1.7	2.3	1.6	1.9	2.1	0.2	1.6	2.1	0.9	1.5	2.7	0.7	1.8
8. Amphetamines	2.5	0.6	1.6	1.3	0.2	0.7	1.6	0.2	0.9	3.8	0.9	2.4	5.7	3.9	4.9
9. Ecstasy	2.2	0.5	1.3	1.2	0.1	0.6	1.8	0.1	0.9	3.1	0.6	1.9	4.2	2.9	3.7
10. Hallucinogens (total)	3.5	0.9	2.2	2.4	0.2	1.2	2.8	0.8	1.8	4.6	1.4	3.0	6.1	2.2	4.2
11. LSD	2.2	0.3	1.3	1.3	0.1	0.8	1.7	0.2	0.9	2.7	0.5	1.7	5.3	1.8	3.7
12. Other Hallucinogens (specify)	2.8	0.6	1.7	2.2	0.1	1.1	2.3	0.7	1.4	3.7	1.1	2.3	3.0	0.7	2.0
13. Hypnotics and Sedatives (total)	1.8	1.1	1.4	1.2	0.4	0.8	1.4	1.4	1.4	2.2	1.5	1.9	2.7	1.1	2.1
14. Benzodiacepines															
15. Other Medic. (specify)															
16. Solvents	8.0	3.7	4.8	4.5	1.6	2.9	6.7	4.6	5.7	6.7	0.5	5.9	5.3	2.5	4.1
17. Steroids															
13. Other															

M = Male; F = Female; T= Total

167

TABLE 4.3 *cont'd.*

Study Details Reference:	Irish Health Behaviours in Schools Survey, Centre for Health Promotion Studies, NUI Galway. Not yet published.
Year	1998
Single/Repeated Study	Single, to be repeated in 2002
Context (health/crime /drugs only…)	Health behaviours and perceptions
Area Covered	National: Republic of Ireland - 26 counties
Type of School	All
Age Range	9-17 included here
Data Collection Procedure	Self-completed questionnaire
Sample Size	8,497
Sampling Frame	School, primary and post-primary from Department of Education & Science lists
Sampling Procedures	Two-stage random sample, within Health Board regions and classrooms
Oversampled Groups	None
Weighting Procedures	None applied here
Absents of School at the Time of Survey	6% in primary schools, 14% in post-primary schools
Response Rate (M,F,T)	92% of primary schools, 86% of post-primary schools. Total, including absentees = 73%. Gender breakdown not available.

TABLE 4.3 *cont'd.*

Definitions Drugs Definitions:	Description of what is included in each drug category
1. Any Illegal Drugs	Tranquilisers or sedatives, amphetamine, LSD, cocaine, heroin, ecstasy, solvents, magic mushrooms
2. Cannabis	Marijuana (grass, pot) or cannabis (hash, hash oil)
3. Opiates (Total)	
4. Heroin	Heroin (smack, skag)
5. Other Opiates (Specify)	
5. Cocaine (Total, including Crack)	Cocaine (coke, crack)
8. Amphetamines	Amphetamines (speed, whizz)
9. Ecstasy	(E, XTC)
10. Hallucinogens (Total)	LSD and magic mushrooms
11. LSD	LSD (acid, trips)
12. Other Hallucinogens (Specify)	Magic mushrooms (pucal, mushies)
13. Hypnotics and Sedatives (Total)	Tranquilisers or sedatives without prescription (barbs, downers, jellies)
14. Benzodiacepines	
15. Other Medic. (Specify)	
16. Solvents	Solvents (e.g. glue, gas)
17. Steroids	
18. Other (Specify)	

TABLE 4.4
School Surveys on Drug Use. Results, Study Details and Definitions.
Health Behaviours of School Pupils in the Eastern Health Board. Prevalence.

Empty Cells indicate 'no information available'

COUNTRY Ireland			LIFETIME PREVALENCE (%) Age Groups														
DRUGS (Important: see 'drug definitions' in the Methodology box.)	Total Sample			11-12			13-14			15-16			17-18				
	10-18																
	M	F	T	M	F	T	M	F	T	M	F	T	M	F	T		
1. Any Illegal Drugs																	
2. Cannabis	25.9	14.5	20.5														
3. Opiates (total)																	
4. Heroin	1.9	0.4	1.1														
5. Other Opiates (specify)																	
5. Cocaine (total, including crack)	2.8	1.2	2.0														
8. Amphetamines	6.3	2.8	4.6														
9. Ecstasy	4.6	1.6	3.1														
10. Hallucinogens (total)																	
11. LSD	4.8	1.7	3.3														
12. Other Hallucinogens (specify)	7.4	2.5	5.1														
13. Hypnotics and Sedatives (total)	3.7	3.0	3.3														
14. Benzodiacepines																	
15. Other Medic. (specify)																	
16. Solvents	15.1	9.9	12.6														
17. Steroids																	
13. Other																	

M = Male; F = Female; T= Total

TABLE 4.4 *cont'd.*

COUNTRY Ireland DRUGS (Important: see 'drug definitions' in the Methodology box.)	Total Sample			LAST 12 MONTHS PREVALENCE (%) Age Groups												
	10-18			11-12			13-14			15-16			17-18		
	M	F	T	M	F	T	M	F	T	M	F	T	M	F	T
1. Any Illegal Drugs															
2. Cannabis															
3. Opiates (total)															
4. Heroin															
5. Other Opiates (specify)															
5. Cocaine (total, including crack)															
8. Amphetamines															
9. Ecstasy															
10. Hallucinogens (total)															
11. LSD															
12. Other Hallucinogens (specify)															
13. Hypnotics and Sedatives (total)															
14. Benzodiacepines															
15. Other medic. (specify)															
16. Solvents															
17. Steroids															
13. Other															

M = Male; F = Female; T= Total

TABLE 4.4 *cont'd.*

LAST 30 DAYS PREVALENCE (%)

COUNTRY Ireland DRUGS (Important: see 'drug definitions' in the Methodology box.)	Total Sample 10-18			Age Groups 11-12			13-14			15-16			17-18		
	M	F	T	M	F	T	M	F	T	M	F	T	M	F	T
1. Any Illegal Drugs															
2. Cannabis	14.4	6.2	10.5												
3. Opiates (total)															
4. Heroin**	1.3	0.5	0.9												
5. Other Opiates (specify)															
5. Cocaine (total, including crack)**	2.1	0.8	1.5												
8. Amphetamines**	4.5	2.0	3.4												
9. Ecstasy**	4.2	1.4	2.9												
10. Hallucinogens (total)															
11. LSD**	2.7	1.2	2.0												
12. Other Hallucinogens (specify)**	4.7	1.5	3.2												
13. Hypnotics and Sedatives (total)**	2.0	1.9	1.9												
14. Benzodiacepines															
15. Other Medic. (specify)															
16. Solvents**	8.7	5.3	7.1												
17. Steroids															
13. Other															

M = Male; F = Female; T= Total
** post primary schools only

TABLE 4.4 *cont'd.*

Study Details Reference:	Rhatigan, A. & Shelley, E. (1999) *Health Behaviours of School Pupils in the Eastern Health Board.* Dublin: Eastern Health Board.
Year	1998
Single/Repeated Study	Single
Context (health/crime/ drugs only....)	Health
Area Covered	Primary and post-primary schools
Type of School	10-17 year olds
Age Range	9-17 included here
Data Collection	Procedure Self-completed questionnaire (based on WHO Health Behaviour in school-aged children questionnaire)
Sample Size	6,081
Sampling Frame	Schools list
Sampling Procedures	A random sample of schools stratified by county and by school type (the latter in the case of post-primary schools only)
Oversampled Groups	None
Weighting Procedures	None
Absents of School at the Time of Survey	Pupils absent (n=674); refused(n=24); parental consent not given (n=264)
Response Rate (M,F,T)	T=78.2%. Gender not reported

TABLE 4.4 *cont'd.*

Definitions	
Drugs Definitions:	Description of what is included in each drug category
1. Any Illegal Drugs	Not reported
2. Cannabis	Cannabis or marijuana
3. Opiates (Total)	Not reported
4. Heroin	Heroin (smack, skag)
5. Other Opiates (Specify)	Not reported
5. Cocaine (Total, including Crack)	Cocaine (coke, crack)
8. Amphetamines	Amphetamines (speed, whizz)
9. Ecstasy	Ecstasy (E, XTC) 1
0. Hallucinogens (Total)	Not reported
11. LSD	LSD (acid, trips)
12. Other Hallucinogens (Specify)	Magic mushrooms (pucal, mushies)
13. Hypnotics and Sedatives (Total)	Tranquilisers, sedatives, barbs, downers, jellies, (without a doctor's prescription).
14. Benzodiacepines	Not reported separately
15. Other Medic. (Specify)	Not reported
16. Solvents	Solvents (glue, gas)
17. Steroids	Not reported
18. Other (Specify)	Drugs by injection with a needle

TABLE 4.5

Treated Drug Misuse 1990-1999. Characteristics of Clients.

All Contacts Starting Treatment.

Country Ireland 1995–1999. Dublin 1990–1994 Characteristics	1990*	1991*	1992*	1993*	1994*	1995	1996	1997	1998	1999
No. of all treatment cases/demands	1575	1722	1931	2043	2250	3609	3924	3879	5081	4277
Sex distr. Male (%) / Female (%)	76/24	78/22	78/22	78/22	81/19	80/20	73/27	70/30	71/29	70/30
Mean Age (years)	25	25.3	24.7	23.7	22.8	22.6	22.8	23.6	24.3	24.6
Age Distribution (%) <15	1	1.7	2	1.2	2.1	1.3	1	0.8	0.7	0.7
15-19	17.6	15.7	20.1	26.4	33.4	35.8	34	28.6	23.9	21
20-24	32.2	28.8	31.2	34.4	33.3	35.7	36.4	35.6	35.8	36.9
25-29	29.4	31.6	25.2	21.2	17.1	14.6	14.7	18.4	20.6	22
30-34	12.9	14.2	14.6	10.7	9.8	7.2	8.7	10.3	10.6	10.8
35-39	4.7	5.5	5	3.9	3	3	3.2	4.1	5.3	5.6
40-44	1.5	1.5	1.3	1.7	0.8	1.4	1.3	1.2	1.8	1.7
45-49	0.2	0.8	0.3	0.2	0.4	0.5	0.7	0.7	0.8	0.7
50-54	0.2	0.1	0.2	0	0.1	0.3	0.1	0.1	0.3	0.4
55-59	0.1	0	0.1	0	0	0.1	0.1	0.1	0.1	0.1
60-64	0.1	0.1	0	0	0	0.1	0	0.1	0.1	0.1
>=65	0	0	0	0	0	0.1	0	0.1	0	0
Number of cases with missing inform on age	36	33	13	10	15	19	10	15	18	20
Currently injecting any drug (%)	53.1	50.4	51.8	50.8	46	32.4	31.8	38.1	36.7	34.4
Ever injected any drug but not currently (%)	24.2	23.1	17.4	17.1	18.1	16.5	16	18.8	23.5	24.9
Ever injected any drug (%)	78.4	75.8	70	68.9	64.7	50.5	48.8	58.7	63.4	61.7
IV route of admin. main drug (%)	66.3	59.9	56.8	57.8	55.3	39.4	36.9	45.3	48.7	48.8

* Dublin refers to Greater Dublin Area

TABLE 4.5 *cont'd.*

Main/primary drug (%) – (% IV use)	1990* dr. % (IV%)	1991* dr. % (IV%)	1992* dr. % (IV%)	1993* dr. % (IV%)	1994* dr. % (IV%)	1995 dr. % (IV%)	1996 dr. % (IV%)	1997 dr. % (IV%)	1998 dr. % (IV%)	1999 dr. % (IV%)
Opiates (Total)	78.2 (84)	75.1 (79)	72.8 (77)	77.3 (75)	80.5 (69)	72.1 (55)	76.9 (48)	77.2 (59)	78.8 (62)	73.3 (66)
Heroin	34.6 (88)	34.9 (85)	35.0 (78)	49.3 (76)	59.0 (69)	62.1 (54)	71.3 (49)	69.0 (64)	70.8 (67)	68.6 (69)
Methadone (any)	1.7 (16)	3.5 (5)	4.7 (3)	5.2 (1)	4.8 (12)	3.4 (0)	2.9 (0)	6.4 (5)	5.6 (4)	3.1 (11)
Other Opiates	41.8 (83)	36.7 (81)	33.0 (86)	22.8 (89)	16.7 (84)	6.6 (89)	2.6 (74)	1.8 (57)	1.7 (69)	1.7 (51)
Cocaine (Total)	0.7 (18)	0.4 (0)	0.5 (30)	0.3 (0)	0.4 (13)	0.5 (6)	0.6 (9)	1.0 (11)	1.6 (11)	1.2 (14)
Cocaine ClH	0.7 (18)	0.4 (0)	0.5 (33)	0.3 (0)	0.3 (17)	0.5 (6)	0.6 (9)	0.9 (11)	1.5 (11)	1.1 (15)
Crack	0	0	0.1 (0)	0	0.1 (0)	0	0	0	0	0
Stimulants (Total)	0.3 (0)	0.8 (8)	3.3 (2)	5.1 (2)	3.3 (1)	8.0 (0)	6.5 (0)	7.1 (0)	4.9 (0)	6.4 (2)
Amphetamines	0.3 (0)	0.5 (13)	0.5 (0)	0.6 (17)	0.5 (9)	0.4 (7)	0.4 (7)	1.3 (0)	1.4 (2)	1.4 (10)
MDMA and derivatives	0	0.3 (0)	2.8 (2)	4.4 (0)	2.8 (0)	7.4 (0)	6.0 (0)	5.8 (0)	3.6 (0)	4.9 (0)
Other Stimulants	0	0	0	0	0	0.2 (0)	0.1 (0)	0	0	0
Hypnot. and sedat. (Total)	3.8 (7)	5.2 (0)	3.7 (11)	2.8 (0)	1.6 (6)	2.3 (1)	1.5 (2)	1.7 (3)	2.1 (2)	1.4 (0)
Barbiturates	0	0.3 (0)	0	0.1 (0)	0	0.1 (33)	0	0	0	0
Benzodiacepines	3.6 (7)	4.7 (0)	3.5 (12)	2.2 (0)	1.5 (6)	1.8 (0)	0.9 (3)	1.3 (2)	1.8 (2)	1.1 (0)
Others	0.1 (0)	0.2 (0)	0.3 (0)	0.6 (0)	0.1 (0)	0.4 (0)	0.6 (0)	0.4 (7)	0.3 (0)	0.2 (0)
Hallucinogens (Total)	0.3 (20)	0.8 (8)	1.4 (4)	2.1 (2)	1.8 (0)	1.4 (0)	0.4 (6)	0.6 (0)	0.3 (0)	0.2 (0)
LSD	0.3 (20)	0.7 (8)	1.4 (4)	2.1 (2)	1.4 (0)	1.1 (0)	0.4 (6)	0.6 (0)	0.3 (0)	0.2 (0)
Others	0	0.1 (0)	0	0.1 (0)	0.3 (0)	0.3 (0)	0	0	0	0
Volatile Inhalants (total)	2.4 (0)	2.5 (0)	2.5 (0)	0.9 (0)	0.9 (0)	0.7 (0)	0.6 (0)	0.6 (0)	0.7 (0)	0.6 (0)
Cannabis (Total)	13.4 (1)	14.5 (1)	15.3 (1)	11.4 (0)	11.5 (0)	14.9 (0)	13.4 (0)	11.8 (0)	12.1 (0)	16.6 (0)
Others Substance (Total)	0.8 (8)	0.6 (0)	0.5 (11)	0.3 (0)	0.1 (0)	0.2 (0)	0.1 (0)	0	0.1 (0)	0.3 (0)
No. Inpatient / Residential UNITS reporting	3	2	2	2	2	5	11	18	18	17
No. Outpatient / Nonresidential UNITS repo.	8	9	10	10	11	13	31	45	76	75
No. Low threshold UNITS reporting	1	1	1	0	0	2	1	2	6	7
No. General Practitioners reporting	1	1	0	0	0	4	4	0	1	32
No. Treatment Unit in Prison UNITS reporting	3	2	2	1	1	2	1	0	0	2

(1) Residential, non-residential (very good coverage); GPs (1990-1998, poor coverage); prisons (poor coverage); 1999, good coverage). The incorporation of GPs was greatly improved in 1999. It is important to note that some units treat a small number of clients.
* Dublin refers to Greater Dublin Area

TABLE 4.6

Treated Drug Misuse 1990-1999. Characteristics of Clients.

First Contacts Starting Treatment.

Country Ireland 1995–199. Dublin 1990–1994 Characteristics	1990*	1991*	1992*	1993*	1994*	1995	1996	1997	1998	1999
No. of first treatment cases/demands	624	450	668	859	1150	1870	2014	1465	1621	1636
Sex distr. Male (%) / Female (%)	75/25	81/19	79/21	80/20	83/17	80/20	73/27	72/28	74/26	73/27
Mean Age (years)	22.8	21.9	21.5	21.1	20.6	21.1	21.3	22	22.1	22.7
Age Distribution (%) <15	2.3	5.4	5.1	2.3	3.5	2.4	1.7	1.6	1.6	1.5
15-19	33.1	34.9	37	42.4	47.8	45.9	44.1	38.3	36.5	32.2
20-24	33.6	34.2	35.8	36.6	32.8	33.7	34.8	36.5	36.2	38.2
25-29	17.5	14.4	12.8	11.9	9.3	10.7	11.3	14	15.8	16.3
30-34	7.8	7	53.7	4.2	5	4	4.5	5.3	5.4	6.4
35-39	3.6	2.3	2.7	1.8	1.2	1.7	2.2	2.7	2.6	3.2
40-44	1.6	0.5	0.5	0.4	0.3	0.9	0.8	1	0.9	1.3
45-49	0	0.9	0.3	0	0.1	0.3	0.5	0.3	0.4	0.3
50-54	0.2	0.2	0.2	0	0.1	0.3	0.1	0.1	0.4	0.3
55-59	0.2	0	0	0	0	0.1	0	0	0.1	0.1
60-64	0	0.2	0	0	0	0	0	0.1	0.1	0.2
>=65	0.2	0	0	0	0	0.1	0	0.1	0	0
Number of cases with missing inform on age	8	6	3	2	5	6	2	5	4	10
Currently injecting any drug (%)	38.7	31.3	31.7	38.8	36.8	19.8	20.9	24.6	22.8	22.7
Ever injected any drug but not currently (%)	17.7	11.9	9.5	11.4	15.4	10.9	10.8	11	12	15.2
Ever injected any drug (%)	58.9	44.2	41.7	50.8	52.5	32	32.1	36.8	37.2	39.3
IV route of admin. main drug (%)	48.3	36.2	33.9	44.1	46.7	23.8	24.3	29.3	28.8	30.6

* Dublin only

TABLE 4.6 contd.

Main/primary drug (%) – (% IV use)	1990* dr. % (IV%)	1991* dr. % (IV%)	1992* dr. % (IV%)	1993* dr. % (IV%)	1994* dr. % (IV%)	1995 dr. % (IV%)	1996 dr. % (IV%)	1997 dr. % (IV%)	1998 dr. % (IV%)	1999 dr. % (IV%)
Opiates (total)	61.1 (78)	49.0 (73)	48.9 (67)	64.0 (69)	74.7 (62)	60.5 (39)	65.5 (37)	61.2 (48)	59.8 (48)	55.4 (55)
Heroin	22.1 (83)	24.0 (74)	26.3 (61)	46.2 (67)	59.0 (63)	54.5 (38)	63.1 (37)	58.6 (49)	56.3 (50)	53.2 (56)
Methadone (any)	1.2 (29)	1.1 (20)	1.4 (0)	2.6 (0)	3.7 (12)	2.2 (0)	1.3 (0)	1.7 (4)	2.5 (3)	1.2 (15)
Other Opiates	37.6 (77)	23.8 (75)	21.2 (79)	15.2 (85)	12.0 (77)	3.8 (87)	1.2 (48)	0.8 (50)	1.0 (50)	1.1 (39)
Cocaine (total)	1.0 (0)	1.1 (0)	0.6 (50)	0.4 (0)	0.3 (0)	0.5 (0)	0.8 (6)	1.4 (0)	2.0 (0)	1.6 (8)
Cocaine CIH	1.0 (0)	1.1 (0)	0.6 (50)	0.4 (0)	0.3 (0)	0.5 (0)	0.8 (7)	1.4 (0)	1.9 (0)	1.6 (8)
Crack	0	0	0	0	0	0	0.1 (0)	0	0.1 (0)	0
Stimulants (total)	0.5 (0)	1.1 (0)	5.9 (3)	8.6 (1)	4.1 (0)	11.6 (0)	10.4 (1)	13. 1(0)	9.6 (0)	11.0 (1)
Amphetamines	0.5 (0)	0.7 (0)	0.2 (0)	0.7 (17)	0.5 (0)	0.4 (0)	0.6 (8)	2.2 (0)	2.3 (0)	2.1 (6)
MDMA and derivatives	0	0.5 (0)	5.7 (3)	7.9 (0)	3.6 (0)	11.0 (0)	9.6 (0)	10.8 (0)	7.3 (0)	8.8 (0)
Other Stimulants	0	0	0	0	0	0.2 (0)	0.2 (0)	0.1 (0)	0.1 (0)	0
Hypnot. and sedat. (total)	5.7 (9)	5.5 (0)	4.5 (3)	2.6 (0)	1.0 (0)	1.8 (0)	1.1 (0)	1.7 (0)	1.9 (0)	1.0 (0)
Barbiturates	0	0.5 (0)	0	0	0	0.1 (0)	0	0	0	0
Benzodiacepines	5.0 (9)	4.8 (0)	4.2 (4)	2.0 (0)	0.8 (0)	1.1 (0)	0.7 (0)	1.3 (0)	1.5 (0)	0.8 (0)
Others	0.3 (0)	0.2 (0)	0.3 (0)	0.6 (0)	0.2 (0)	0.7 (0)	0.5 (0)	0.5 (0)	0.4 (0)	0.2 (0)
Hallucinogens (total)	0.5 (0)	1.8 (0)	2.4 (0)	3.6 (0)	2.3 (0)	1.9 (0)	0.5 (0)	0.8 (0)	0.4 (0)	0.2 (0)
LSD	0.5 (0)	1.6 (0)	2.4 (0)	3.6 (0)	1.7 (0)	1.6 (0)	0.5 (0)	0.8 (0)	0.4 (0)	0.2 (0)
Others	0	0.2 (0)	0	0	0.5 (0)	0.3 (0)	0	0	0	0.1 (0)
Volatile inhalants (total)	4.7 (0)	6.6 (0.0)	5.4 (0)	1.6 (0)	1.1 (0)	1.0 (0)	0.9 (0)	0.8 (0)	1.4 (0)	1.2 (0)
Cannabis (total)	25.4 (0.7)	34.1 (0.7)	30.9 (1)	18.6 (0)	16.3 (1)	22.4 (0)	20.7 (0)	21.0 (0)	24.7 (0)	29.4 (0)
Others substance (total)	1.2 (0)	0.7 (0)	1.4 (11)	0.6 (0)	0.3 (0)	0.2 (0)	0.1 (0)	0	0.3 (0)	0.2 (0)
Nr. Inpatient / Residential UNITS reporting	2	2	2	2	2	5	10	13	16	12
Nr. Outpatient / Nonresidential UNITS repo.	8	7	9	10	11	13	29	40	72	69
Nr. Low threshold UNITS reporting	1	1	1	0	0	2	1	1	2	4
Nr. General Practitioners reporting	1	0	0	0	0	4	3	0	1	19
Nr. Treatment Unit in Prison UNITS reporting	3	2	1	1	1	2	1	0	0	2

* Dublin only

TABLE 4.7

Price in Euros at Street Level of Some Illegal Substances. 1995–1999.

Empty Cells indicate 'no information available'

NAME OF THE SOURCE:	Garda National Drugs Unit														
COUNTRY	Ireland														
Year	1995			1996			1997			1998			1999		
	Min.	Max.	Average	Min.	Max.	Average	Min.	Max.	Average	Min.	Max.	Average	Min.	Max.	Average
Cannabis resin (per gram)			13			13			13			13			13
Cannabis leaves (per gram)			3			3			3			3			3
Heroin brown (per gram)	100	300	190	100	300	190	100	300	190	100	300	190	100	300	190
Heroin white (per gram)															
Cocaine powder (per gram)			102			102			102			102			102
Crack (per rock)															
Amphetamines powder (per gram)	10	13	12	10	13	12	10	13	12	10	13	12	10	13	12
'Ecstasy' (per tablet)	19	25	22	10	15	13	10	15	13	10	13	12	10	13	12
LSD (per dose)	10	15	13	10	15	13	10	15	13	10	15	13	10	15	13

Study Details

Type of Study:	Ad hoc - estimations of street prices by Gardaí
Geographical	
Sampling Frame:	Coverage: Local (Dublin prices - number of sites covered not known)
Sampling Bias:	Street work by Gardaí
	Garda intervention
Price Reported by:	Law enforcement agency - Gardaí
Method of Estimation:	User's report to Garda street workers
Source References:	Personal communication - Gardaí
Bibliographic References:	Personal communication - Gardaí

APPENDIX 5

QUANTITY OF DRUGS SEIZURES – IRELAND

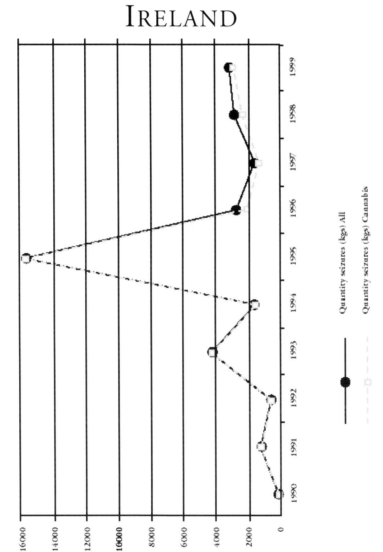

FIGURE 5.1

Ireland 1990–1999. Quantity of Drugs Seizures. Kilograms.

Quantity seizures (kgs) All

Quantity seizures (kgs) Cannabis

Source: Annual Reports of An Garda Síochána

APPENDIX 6

REGIONAL HEALTH BOARD AREAS – IRELAND

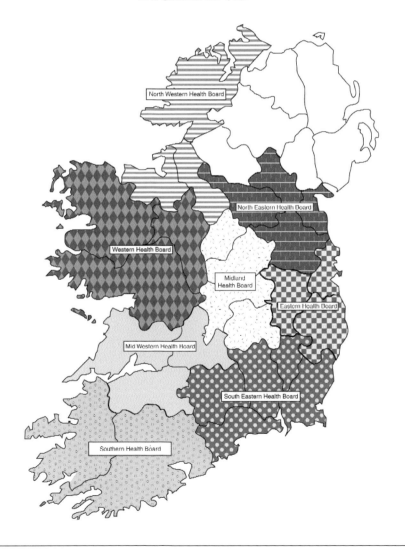

Notes on Authors and the Drug Misuse Research Division

Rosalyn Moran, MA, MSc, HDE

Rosalyn Moran is a research psychologist. She has conducted and managed social research in national, European and international contexts and in public and private-sector environments. She worked on the development of the Framework Programme for European Research and Development as an expert to the European Commission. She has published broadly in health and related areas. Currently, she heads the Mental Health Research Division at the Health Research Board.

Email address: rmoran@hrb.ie

Mary O'Brien BA, DipStats, DipSoc&SocRes

Mary O'Brien is a senior social researcher. She is responsible for the co-ordination of the National Drug Treatment Reporting System. She is the DMRD representative on national and European fora in relation to epidemiology of drug misuse, drug treatment demand, and drug-related deaths. She is a member of a national committee on joint action against new synthetic drugs. Current research includes analysis of trends in drug misuse in Ireland and population survey work. She authors annual reports on treated drug misuse in Ireland.

Email address: mary@hrb.ie

Lucy Dillon, BA

Lucy Dillon is a sociologist. She has carried out research in the areas of crisis pregnancy, methadone maintenance treatment and drug use in prison. She has expertise in the area of drug-related infectious diseases and drug use in the context of the criminal justice system.

Email address: lucy@hrb.ie

Eimear Farrell, BA, MSc

Eimear Farrell is a research psychologist. She has previously been involved in research in the field of education in Ireland and research into pathological gambling. She carried out research on perceptions of drug-related services while in the DMRD. In September 2000 she began a full-time doctorate on the clinical psychology programme in University College Dublin.

Paula Mayock, BEd, MEd

Paula Mayock is a researcher at the Addiction Research Centre, Trinity College, Dublin. She has carried out research on drug use by young people and is continuing work in this area. She has also conducted an exploratory study on cocaine use in Ireland and will be undertaking further work on this topic as part of a European-wide study.
Email address: pmayock@tcd.ie

The Drug Misuse Research Division of the Health Research Board

The Drug Misuse Research Division (DMRD) was responsible for researching and compiling this overview. The DMRD is a division of the Health Research Board (HRB), based in Dublin, and is involved in national and international research and information activities in relation to drugs and their misuse. The DMRD is funded by national and EU sources and contract research. International collaborators include the EMCDDA and Council of Europe Pompidou Group.

The DMRD maintains and develops the national epidemiological database on treated drug misuse in Ireland – the National Drug Treatment Recording System (NDTRS). The NDTRS provides comprehensive data on the numbers and characteristics of those treated for drug misuse in Ireland.

Current and recently completed research studies include research into trends in drug misuse; knowledge, attitudes and beliefs regarding drugs and drug users; drug service provision; crèche availability and use in drug treatment contexts; drug use, impaired driving and traffic accidents; drug use by prisoners and drug use in rural areas.

The DMRD is involved in information and dissemination activities at national and European levels. It publishes DrugNet Ireland. A new National Documentation Centre is being established in the DMRD as an initiative of the National Advisory Committee on Drugs (NACD).

HEALTH RESEARCH BOARD
PUBLICATIONS SINCE 1997

Browne, C., Daly, A. & Walsh, D. (1999). *Activities of Irish Psychiatric Services 1997.* Dublin: The Health Research Board.

Browne, C., Daly, A. & Walsh, D. (2000). *Activities of Irish Psychiatric Services 1998.* Dublin: The Health Research Board.

Bryan, A., Moran, R., Farrell, E. & O'Brien, M. (2000). *Drug-Related Knowledge, Attitudes and Beliefs in Ireland: Report of a nation-wide survey.* Dublin: Drug Misuse Research Division, The Health Research Board.

Daly, A. & Walsh, D. (2000). *Activities of Irish Psychiatric Services 1999.* Dublin: The Health Research Board.

Dillon, L. (2001). *Drug Use among Prisoners: An exploratory study.* Dublin: The Health Research Board.

Health Research Board (1998). *Annual Report and Accounts, 1997.* Dublin: The Health Research Board.

Health Research Board (1999). *Annual Report and Accounts, 1998.* Dublin: The Health Research Board.

Health Research Board (2000). *Making Knowledge Work for Health: Towards a strategy for research and innovation for health.* Dublin: The Health Research Board.

Keogh, F., Roche, A. & Walsh, D. (1999). *'We Have No Beds….': An enquiry into the availability and use of acute psychiatric beds in the Eastern Health Board region.* Dublin: The Health Research Board.

Keogh, F. & Walsh, D. (1997). *Activities of Irish Psychiatric Services 1996.* Dublin: The Health Research Board.

Moran, R. (1999). *The Availability, Use and Evaluation of the Provision of Crèche Facilities in Association with Drug Treatment.* Dublin: Drug Misuse Research Division, The Health Research Board.

Moran, R., O'Brien, M. & Duff, P. (1997) *Treated Drug Misuse in Ireland: National report 1996.* Dublin: Drug Misuse Research Division, The Health Research Board.

Mulvany, F. (2000). *Annual Report of the National Intellectual Disability Database Committee 1998/1999.* Dublin: The Health Research Board.

National Intellectual Disability Database Committee (1997). *Annual Report 1996.* Dublin: The Health Research Board.

O'Brien, M. & Moran, R. (1997). *Overview of Drug Issues in Ireland: A resource document.* Dublin: Drug Misuse Research Division, The Health Research Board.

O'Brien, M., Moran, R., Kelleher, T. & Cahill, P. (2000). *National Drug Treatment Reporting System. Statistical Bulletin 1997 & 1998. National Data and Data by Health Board.* Dublin: The Health Research Board.

O'Brien, A., Moran, R. & O'Brien, M. (2001). *Annotated Bibliography of Drug Misuse in Ireland.* Dublin: Drug Misuse Research Division, The Health Research Board.

O'Higgins, K. & Duff, P. (1997) *Treated Drug Misuse in Ireland: First national report.* Dublin: The Health Research Board.

INDEX

This index lists the organisations, programmes and initiatives, and drugs of misuse mentioned in the text. It does not cover subject areas and issues, such as demand reduction, health matters, or social issues. These may be accessed through consulting the Contents on pages v to viii.